# Better Badminton for all
## (NEW EDITION)

## J. C. DOWNEY

**PELHAM BOOKS**

First published in Great Britain by
PELHAM BOOKS LTD
52 Bedford Square
London WC1B 3EF
1969
New Edition 1975
Second impression March 1977

0720714389

ISBN 0 7207 0862 1

Printed in Great Britain by
Redwood Burn Limited, Trowbridge & Esher
and bound by Dorstel Press, Harlow

# CONTENTS

3

## PART THREE – TEACHING BADMINTON

## PART FOUR – COMPETITION BADMINTON

# ILLUSTRATIONS
*between pages 48 and 49*

## ACKNOWLEDGEMENTS

I would like to express my thanks to the following:

All the young players who unknowingly have assisted me in developing the ideas expressed in this book.

The Badminton Association of England for permission to print the Laws of the Game.

Mr R. Cardigan for his illustrations.

Mrs Nancy Horner who has given me invaluable assistance and advice from the beginning.

Finally, my wife, who has patiently tolerated my absence during the evenings spent in writing this book.

J.C.D.

# FOREWORD

by Nancy Horner
The Hon. Director of Coaching of
The Badminton Association of England

When you first dip into this book, you will probably straight away feel that it has been written by an expert. You will be right. Jake Downey knows the game of badminton inside out, both from the the playing and teaching angle, having, on the one hand, played in first class badminton circles and, on the other, taught the game in school and college for a number of years.

As a very young man he showed great promise as a player and played for Middlesex County team. He had the potential to have perhaps played for England, but a serious accident on an autobahn in Germany (from which he was obviously lucky to come out alive) caused sufficient damage to a leg virtually to finish all propects of reaching the heights. By dint of carrying out a systematic programme of exercises he has managed several years later to strengthen the leg and to reach a considerable degree of fitness. Instead of playing in competitions he decided to concentrate his energies on coaching young players. Among the players he has coached have been the 1973 All England Ladies singles champion, Margaret Beck; the 1974 Commonwealth Games and European Championships triple champion, and All England Ladies singles finalist, Gillian Gilks; the 1974/5 English National singles champion, Paul Whetnall; and the 1972 and 1975 England Uber Cup teams.

His education and background have fitted him well on the teaching side. This includes a course of three years studying at Loughborough College of Physical Education and one year studying Movement at the Laban Art of Movement Centre. He has also acquired the Academic Diploma in Education at the University of London, and the M.Ed. in Philosophy of Education at the University of Manchester. He has been a teacher in London, and is now a Senior Lecturer in Physical Education at Wall Hall College, Herts.

Jake Downey has unbounding energy and enthusiasm for the subject on which he is currently engaged, and I know, for I have talked with him at various stages in its development, that he has put a great deal of thought into the writing of this book.

He has divided it into four main parts – the basic strokes and tactics of the game for the beginner and inexperienced player, practices aimed at the improving player to give him finesse, strength and endurance, and finally a section for the teacher, particularly the one who wishes to take the game in school and has little knowledge and a fairly low standard of play himself. In all these branches Jake has tried out over a considerable period the methods which he recommends, and his is no theoretical advice, which fails to stand up in practice. What is more, he makes his points in simple terms and useful diagrams, untrammelled with jargon and verbosity.

On the other hand he would be the last one to claim that his suggestions will always work under all conditions and with all people, or that he has said the last word on any subject. In playing and coaching a game conditions will never twice be precisely the same (you only have to consider how you vary as a person yourself on a bleak Monday morning in winter as compared with a glorious summer Saturday afternoon!) Jake Downey is, therefore, throwing out a great variety of ideas to the reader for him to try out, in the hope that these ideas will stimulate further experiments. When you read the last section on teaching the game, you will find that he is at great pains to make his pupils experiment for themselves as to how best to carry out certain tasks, and does not advocate their slavishly copying a demonstration carried out by the teacher. A great believer in the joy of discovery, in the same way he wants his reader to experiment for himself, but, of course, gives him copious ideas to help him.

There is a wealth of information for everyone in this book, and so far as I am aware, the material in sections 2 and 3 have never before been presented in this form where badminton is concerned. In particular physical fitness as it pertains to the game, pressure training and practices related to the games situation have not been covered as they are here. I commend this book to all followers of badminton – young and old, beginner or international, teacher or coach.

In this new edition of *Better Badminton for All* Jake Downey has added a fourth section on 'Competition Badminton'. This is an interesting subject for players and coaches at all levels, as club matches can be just as fierce and as competitive as international ties, and the author presents his ideas simply and clearly as in the rest of the book. The result should stimulate followers of the game to further efforts, and open up fresh avenues to them.

Nancy Horner

# INTRODUCTION

Anyone can learn to play Badminton. The outstanding advantage Badminton has over all other racket games is the early satisfaction it gives to the complete beginner. Very little skill is required to hit the shuttlecock over the net and play a rally with a friend. The very nature of the equipment makes this an easy task for the complete beginner. The racket is so light that only a limited amount of strength is required to control it. The design of the shuttlecock is such that it almost floats through the air in its flight. These factors enable any normal healthy child or adult to gain enjoyment at a very early stage in learning the game. One does not have to be an expert to enjoy Badminton as a game.

The opportunities for playing Badminton are numerous. These days it is often introduced as a part of the Physical Education programme in many schools. For the boy or girl who has acquired an interest at school and wishes to play further, there are Youth Clubs, Youth Centres, Church Clubs, etc. which include Badminton as a recreational activity. Many education authorities now provide the opportunity to play in Adult Evening Institutes and Centres of Further Education. Classes are held for beginners as well as players at an advanced level. In general it seems that any building which contains a large hall or a gymnasium usually has a Badminton Court marked out and a group of keen players making use of the facilities.

The game attracts a mixed membership and offers the opportunity for promoting social relationships. It is a healthy active sport which gives enjoyment and satisfaction to everyone. This is derived from the active participation, the mastering of skills, an abundance of physical exercise, the challenge of friendly competition and the promotion of social relationships in a friendly environment.

Though it is a game which can be played as a recreation, even at this level it can demand much mental and physical effort. At the competitive level, it is one of the most demanding of all games; requiring a high level of fitness and a mastery of technique.

The inclusion of Badminton in a school Physical Education programme can be justified in that it requires a mental and physical application in the learning of skills, and the subsequent mastery of bodily movements necessary in the situations which arise in the game. It provides children with healthy enjoyable activity, and fosters good social attitudes, both in social relationships and in establishing obedience and respect for a framework of rules on which the game is founded.

For any beginner the most important considerations are:

It is an attractive game to learn.

It is easy to play and provides a great deal of enjoyment and satisfaction, physically, mentally and socially.

There are many opportunities to play the game and it is a sport in which any beginner will be made welcome.

Having gained enjoyment from playing Badminton at a simple level, there will be a desire to learn more about the game. The keen enthusiast will want to develop even further and may even play at an advanced level and enter competitions. Other players may wish to teach beginners, perhaps start a club and coach the members. The idea of this book is to cater for all those players interested in Badminton. The aim is as the title suggests 'Better Badminton for all'.

The first section provides the essential knowledge necessary to learn the game. As one desires to improve performance, there are techniques to be learnt. These techniques and skills make Badminton one of the fastest of all games. The first section deals with the basic skills of the game and includes information about basic practices and tactics. The second section follows on from this stage. Once the basic skills have been learnt, it is essential to improve them. This section is called 'Training for Badminton'. It contains fitness training programmes and fitness training practices, all related to improving the performance of a player.

The final section, 'Teaching Badminton', is written for the teacher, coach, youth club leader, in fact anyone interested in forming a club and starting the game. The emphasis is on development in the School or Club, with special reference to Group Coaching.

10

PART ONE

# Learning Badminton

# 1. HISTORY AND DEVELOPMENT

There are various accounts of how and when the game of Badminton started. The account usually accepted is that a game with rackets and shuttlecocks was played at the estate of the Duke of Beaufort in Gloucestershire in the 1860s. The estate was called Badminton and hence the game was given the name of Badminton.

From this starting point the game was played in various forms in different countries. In 1877 at Karachi in India the first attempt was made to form a set of rules. The game developed in other areas of the world and it became essential that an acceptable standard set of rules should be devised. In 1893 the Badminton Association of England was formed and a standard set of Laws for the Game were devised. From a membership of a few clubs, this Association now has almost three thousand clubs affiliated to it.

In 1934 the International Badminton Federation was formed, and comprises the associations of all the countries which play Badminton.

In 1899 the first All-England Championships were held. These have developed to the stage when competitors from all over the world arrive to compete in the Championships. Unofficially these Championships are considered to be the World Championships and it is a great honour to compete in them.

Many of the countries affiliated to the International Badminton Federation compete against each other in international matches. Every three years a men's team representing each country competes for the Thomas Cup, which is a much prized trophy presented by Sir George Thomas, the late president of the International Badminton Federation.

Since 1956 the ladies have competed for the Uber Cup in international competition.

Badminton as a game has not received as much publicity as many other sports. The reason for this is that all players are strictly amateur and lack of finance restricts players from travelling to other countries unless as official representatives of their National Associations. Perhaps now that the sport has received greater recognition by its inclusion in the Empire Games, it may yet be considered as an Olympic Sport and receive more interest from the Press and the Public in general.

# 2. EQUIPMENT

### RACKET
A Badminton racket is very light, weighing between 4 oz. to 5½ oz. In selecting

a racket the most important consideration is the 'feel' of the racket. The feel of the racket is dependent upon the size of the grip and the distribution of the weight. A racket may be heavy in the head in relation to the handle, or light in the head in relation to the handle.

Some rackets feel equally balanced in the head and the handle. The weight is distributed evenly. When selecting a racket, try out several until one is found which feels evenly balanced and comfortable to hold.

Many sports' manufacturers now produce a wide range of rackets of various quality. Obviously the quality of the racket affects the price of the racket. The complete beginner is wise to buy a racket at a medium price. With more experience you will make a good choice when selecting the most expensive racket. If you wish to begin with the top quality racket then do so. Any good sports shop will advise you.

Because the racket is so light it can easily be damaged by ill-treatment. When not playing always keep your racket in a press. This prevents the head of the racket warping. Look after your racket and you will receive good service from it.

SHUTTLECOCKS

The shuttlecock is the object used in play. It is referred to as the 'Shuttle' or the 'Bird' or the 'Feather'. It is of a very delicate construction.

A shuttlecock weighs only a small fraction of an ounce. The weight varies between 73 grains weight and 85 grains weight. The weight affects the flight. A shuttlecock varies in speed of flight from slow (73 grains) to fast (85 grains).

It is constructed of 14 to 16 goose feathers inserted into a cork base. The base is covered by kid leather. If the feathers are damaged in any way the flight of the shuttlecock is affected. Always take care of the shuttlecock and smooth out the feathers whenever they become disturbed during play.

SELECTING SHUTTLECOCKS

A shuttle travels slowly in a cold hall and quickly in a warm hall. The speed of flight is affected by the temperature. For this reason select a shuttlecock according to weight, for use in the appropriate temperature.

Shuttlecocks vary in quality. A sports shop will advise you on which quality to buy. If you can afford it always buy the best.

Some firms now manufacture plastic shuttlecocks. Though these are not yet as good as feathered shuttlecocks, they are excellent for practice and much cheaper to buy.

DRESS

Badminton is a fast energetic game requiring a wide range of physical movement. Dress should be chosen for comfort and freedom of movement. White clothing is always worn during play.

FOOTWEAR

The feet receive quite a considerable amount of wear during play. Buy good quality shoes and thick socks to prevent blistering of the feet.

SELECTION

Many firms now manufacture clothing specially designed for Badminton. A good sports shop will stock a large range of clothing and will give expert advice in selection.

ADDITIONAL CLOTHING

For health reasons it is usually sound policy to wear a warm pullover prior to beginning play, and for wear immediately after a game. This helps the body to warm up quickly and prevents cold after a game. As many halls are quite cold many players wear a track suit.

A track suit is really a very sensible purchase and will be found to be extremely useful for play and training.

## 3. OBJECT OF THE GAME

The game is played on a rectangular court, divided into two halves by a net. The game is played by opposing players. Two players make a single game. Four players make a double game. The players occupy opposite halves of the court. The players use rackets to hit the shuttlecock over the net so that it hits the floor on the opponent's side of the court. The doubles court is wider than the singles court.

A contest consists of the best of three games. All games are played up to 15 points or 21 points except Ladies Singles, which are played up to 11 points. At the conclusion of each game, the players change ends. The rules at the end of the book will give more details of the procedure during play.

BEGINNING THE GAME

To begin a contest the players toss. The word 'side' describes the player or pair of players. The side which wins the toss has the chance of:

(*a*) serving first
(*b*) not serving first
(*c*) choice of ends

The side which serves the shuttle is known as the Serving Side. The side which receives the serve is known as the Receiving Side.

SCORING IN THE GAME

Only the serving side can add points to the score. Each side tries to win the service. Having won the service, the side in possession has the opportunity to add points to the score. A point is won during play if a player hits the shuttle to the ground on the opponent's half of the court; or if the opponent is unable to return the shuttle into play. Though a point is won in the way described it is only added to the score if won by the serving side. If the receiving side wins the point, the score remains the same but the receiving side have now won the service. They become known as the Serving Side and have their opportunity to serve and add points to their score. In Doubles play, the receiving side would have to win two rallies before they gained possession of the service.

## 4. ORDER OF SERVICE

THE SINGLES GAME

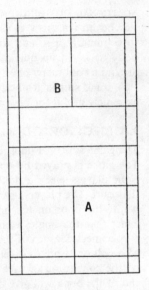

FIG. 1
The game is played by two players, **A** and **B**.
**A** has won the toss and serves first.
The game begins with the score at love-all (0–0).

(1) **A** serves from his right service court diagonally opposite to **B**.
(2) **A** wins the first point. The score becomes 1–0 to **A**.
(3) **A** moves to his left service court to serve diagonally opposite to **B**. The receiver must always stand diagonally opposite to the server.
(4) **A** wins the point. The score becomes 2–0. **A** moves once again to his right service court to serve diagonally opposite to **B**.
(5) **B** wins the next point and wins the service. The score remains the same.
(6) **B** now serves from his right service court diagonally opposite to **A**.
(7) **B** wins the point. The score becomes 1–2. The score of the server is stated first.

It follows that the players stand in the service court related to the score. If the servers' score is an even number the players stand on the right service court. If the servers' score is an odd number the players stand on the left service court.

16

THE DOUBLES GAME

This is slightly more complicated but the principles of changing the service court as a point is won remains the same. At the beginning of the game only one player of the serving side is allowed to serve. He continues to serve until he loses the service to the other side. From then on both players on each side have a turn to serve when their side is in possession of the service. The service always begins from the right court.

Fig. 2

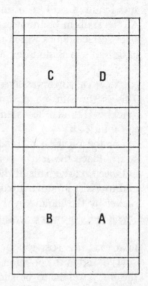

(1) **A** serves diagonally opposite to **C**. The serving side win the point. The score becomes 1–0.

(2) **A** moves to his left court and serves diagonally opposite to **D**. He continues to serve from one player to the other until that serve is lost.

(3) If **A** was serving to **D** before he lost the service, he must remain in that court to receive service until his side gains possession of the service.

(4) Whatever the state of the score, only the serving side may change from one court to the other, in order to serve to each player of the opposing side. The receiving side must remain in the court they occupied before they lost the service.

This is a simple explanation. A more detailed account of order of serving may be referred to in the Laws of the Game (*see* page 221).

## 5. THE SKILLS OF THE GAME

It is possible to play Badminton in a very simple manner without learning more than how to hit the shuttle over the net. This is the game played in its most simple form. Badminton is a game requiring a wide range of movement of the body. It is a fast energetic game with a wide variety of situations occurring in the game. To gain greater enjoyment from the game and to improve performance it is necessary to make progress. Progress is made by the learning of the different techniques and strokes peculiar to the game of Badminton. A player becomes skilled when he has mastered the basic strokes and acquired skill in hitting the shuttle with a variety of different methods. All the skills in Badminton are really common sense. The game has developed a set of techniques which make it easier to play and give better results. The basic skills in Badminton are as follows.

POSITION OF READINESS (*see* Plate 1)
This is the starting position. A player must be alert and ready to move quickly. He must be balanced and in a position to watch his opponent and the shuttlecock.

For the position of readiness stand in the mid-court facing the opposite court. Place the feet a comfortable distance apart with the weight equally balanced on the balls of the feet. Bend the knees slightly to maintain balance and to assist in moving from the spot to any position on the court. Hold the racket by the handle in the hand, and support it lightly at the neck in the free hand. Allow the arms to bend at the elbow and keep the racket head up.

PRACTISE THE POSITION OF READINESS
(1) Stand in the position of readiness. Rock over to the right side and allow the body weight to be supported by the right foot. Pause and rock to the left side so that the weight is supported by the left foot. Return to the ready position, balanced equally on both feet.

Repeat this practice, keeping up a continuous rocking movement before returning to balance on both feet.

In this way, before a player moves off from the spot, he may transfer his weight to the left foot to move to the left. He may transfer weight to the right foot to move to the right. He may place the weight on the right foot to lunge forwards on to his left foot, and the same in moving backwards. The position of readiness is an alert position, weight evenly balanced ready to move off in many different directions.

(2) Stand in the position of readiness. Practise a bouncing action, keeping the feet in contact with the ground. The knees initiate the bounce, by bending and extending. So bounce on the knees. During this movement the upper part of the body should be carried and not allowed to slump. Maintain a light tension in the upper body. The head is upright and looking forwards and the trunk leans slightly forward to assist in balance. The arms are flexed and the racket held with the head up. This is important as most of the strokes

18

are played from a high position, and the racket is ready to move easily and quickly into position.

THE GRIP

The racket should be gripped to give maximum control of the racket face and allow the shuttle to be hit easily from any position. A racket has two faces, both being identical. If the shuttle is hit on the forehand side of the body that face of the racket used to hit the shuttle becomes the forehand face. If the shuttle is hit on the backhand side of the body that face of the racket becomes the backhand face.

FOREHAND GRIP

*Method 1:* Hold the racket by the neck in the left hand. Place the palm of the right hand flat on the strings of the racket. Slide the palm down the racket until the little finger meets the bottom of the handle. Close the fingers and thumb round the handle in a gentle grip. This is the forehand grip.

*Method 2:* Hold the racket by the neck with the left hand. Hold it in front of you, with the head of the racket pointing forwards and the side edge of the racket head pointing towards the ground. Shake hands gently with the handle of the racket. This is the forehand grip.

This grip gives maximum control over the racket face. The fingers can be spread out to allow a more comfortable grip. The more the handle is held in the fingers and not the fist, the greater is the control over the racket face.

THE BACKHAND GRIP

This grip is used to give greater control over the backhand face of the racket and allows ease of movement of the racket on the backhand side of the body.

Stand in the Ready Position. Hold the racket in the forehand grip. Relax the grip and use the left hand to turn the racket slowly to the right until the right thumb lies flat along the back of the handle. Remove the left hand. The racket is now held in the backhand grip. The weight and strength of the thumb is now directly behind the backhand face of the racket.

PRACTICE FOR THE GRIP (*see* Plates 2 and 3)

It is necessary to develop a feel for the correct grip. It is important in the game to be able to take up the correct grip and to be aware of the position of the hand in relation to the handle and the racket face without thinking about it.

Practise spinning the racket in the hand and stop the racket in the correct grip i.e. forehand or backhand grip. When the grip is held correctly by touch and not by looking to see if it is correct, you have developed a 'feel' for the

19

grip. Players must be able to change grip very quickly in the game, so practise until you can change the grip and hold the correct grip at any time.


## 6. THE STROKES—(a) OVERHEAD

Many strokes in Badminton are played from an overhead position. The actual stroke selected from the overhead position is dependent on the position of the player in relation to the court, the shuttlecock and the opposing player. A player may have to move to the rear of the court to play an overhead stroke. From this position he can hit the shuttle high to the back of the opposite court, or smash it down steeply over the net, or drop it over the net. The player may have to make a stroke from an overhead position in the middle of the court. As he is now nearer the net, the opportunity is created for him to smash the shuttle down to the ground in the opponent's court and give the opponent very little chance of returning it. A player may have to run backwards to play a stroke from his backhand side at the rear of the court. He may decide the best shot is a drop shot and so he will play a backhand overhead drop shot. There are numerous possibilities, and understanding of the game will help a player to decide which type of stroke to perform. The essential factor is to be able to perform the particular stroke chosen. The following strokes are all strokes played from an overhead position on the forehand and backhand side. Each stroke involves a preparation, an action and a recovery.

OVERHEAD FOREHAND CLEAR (*see* Plate 4)

This stroke is played from an overhead position on the forehand side. It is usually played from the rear of the court and the aim of the player is to hit the shuttle in a high arc, deep to the rear of the opponent's court.

*Preparation:* Stand in the position of readiness. Hold the racket in the forehand grip with only a light tension in the fingers. Keep the racket head up. Twist the body to the right and step backwards with the right foot so that the left side of the body points towards the net and the weight is supported on the right foot. As the body twists to the right the racket head is taken past your face and allowed to drop behind the right shoulder by bending the elbow and relaxing the right wrist. The wrist is now cocked back. Examine your stance. The body is sideways to the net. The weight is supported by the right foot. The racket is held back in a throwing position with the wrist cocked. The left arm is held high for balance.

*The Action:* As the shuttlecock approaches, begin the throwing action upwards to meet it on impact at racket stretch height above the head. The wrist leads the throwing movement upwards, as the racket head is held back by the cocked wrist. The body weight begins to transfer forwards as the arm straightens out. Just prior to impact the wrist straightens (or uncocks) to bring the racket head forwards at great speed to hit through the shuttlecock. As the shuttle travels forwards after the impact, the racket head follows forwards and downwards across the body in a natural recovery. The weight transfers to the front foot as the arm follows through after the impact with the shuttle, for the player to recover in a balanced position.

BASIC POINTS
  (i) Stand in a sideways position in line with the flight of the shuttle.
 (ii) Prepare for the stroke, weight on the rear foot and racket held back with the wrist cocked.
(iii) Throw upwards to full stretch height and allow the body weight to transfer forwards on to the front foot.
 (iv) Keep both feet in contact with the ground.
  (v) Follow through and recover in a balanced position.
 (vi) These points apply to all the overhead strokes.

There are two types of overhead clear. These are the overhead defensive clear and the attacking clear. The action is the same for both, apart from one difference. The difference is the angle of the racket face at the point of impact. The defensive clear returns the shuttle on a pathway which goes very high and deep in the opposite court. The racket face must be pointing upwards towards this pathway at the moment of impact. It is used to allow a player time to recover when under pressure.

The attacking clear sends the shuttle on a lower pathway just higher than the opponent can reach. It forces the opponent to move quickly to the back of the court, and so play a stroke before the shuttle drops. For this stroke the racket face meets the shuttle at impact at an angle which directs it more forwards than upwards. Both types of clear can be practised by performing the identical action, but altering the angle of the racket face at the moment of impact.

OVERHEAD FOREHAND SMASH (see Plate 5)
The objective of the smash is to hit the shuttle from a high position down to the ground on the opposite court. The shuttle is hit to travel quickly and ˙eeply. For this reason the smash is aimed straight, the shortest distance between two points being a straight line. The racket face must be pointing downwards at the moment of impact, and the racket head must be travelling at great speed to impart force to send the shuttle on its way.

*Stages in the Smash:* Stand in the ready position. The preparation is the same as for the forehand overhead clear. This is a sideways throwing position directly in line with the oncoming shuttle. The wrist is cocked to allow the racket head to drop back.

The throwing action is aimed to meet the shuttle at impact in front of the body in a high position.

21

Begin throwing the racket head up to meet the shuttle. Lead the movement with the wrist, and increase the pressure of the grip on the handle of the racket. As the arm begins to straighten out, allow the wrist to travel forwards (uncock). The racket head is brought forwards at great speed to hit over the top of the shuttle. At the moment of impact the racket face directs the shuttle towards the ground and the wrist whips through as far as it will travel to bring the racket head down over the shuttle. The racket follows through in the direction of the shuttle until the arm naturally falls across the body to recover in a balanced position.

The most difficult part in this stroke is the wrist action which travels through its full range of movement, and the timing of the impact. Practise the stroke in stages.

(1) Preparation or backswing.
(2) The action: a throwing action with the wrist whipping forwards and down.
(3) Recovery: follow through and balance. Do this slowly in stages and then try to join the movements together to make one continuous movement.

### THE OVERHEAD FOREHAND DROP SHOT

There are two types of drop shot from this position. These are the slow drop shot and the fast drop shot.

*The Slow Drop Shot:* From an overhead position the shuttle is hit gently so that it loses speed quickly and drops down close to the net in the opposite court. The drop shot is a very deceptive shot, as the opponent only realises at the last moment that he is receiving a drop shot.

The preparation for the stroke is identical to the preparation for the forehand overhead clear. The point of impact is taken above the head of the player. The racket head is thrown up at the shuttle with the wrist leading the movement. Just prior to impact the speed of the racket head brakes sharply and the movement continues with the face of the racket gently stroking the shuttle softly forwards and upwards. The shuttle travels slightly upwards after impact and then drops steeply over the net. The racket leads the arm in a gentle follow through down and across the body to recover and balance.

Stand in the ready position. Prepare as for a forehand overhead stroke. Throw upwards towards the point of impact above the head. Just before the impact, check the forward movement of the arm and racket to slow the racket down, and continue the movement for the racket face to hit shuttle gently forwards and upwards. Allow the racket to follow through down and across the body still continuing the slow gentle movement.

The later you can delay the checking action of the racket before impact, the greater the deception. Do not stop the racket speed, only slow it down.

22

*The Fast Drop Shot:* This shot carries the shuttle deeper into the court than the slow drop shot. The preparation and throwing action are identical to the slow drop shot. The difference is that the point of impact is high and in front of the body. The racket head is above the shuttle with the racket face pointing downwards at the moment of impact. The racket speed brakes sharply before impact but continues with enough speed to allow the shuttle to pass over the net before it drops quickly to the ground. The racket follows through on its natural arc for the player to recover and balance.

THE OVERHEAD BACKHAND CLEAR (*see* Plate 6)
The shuttle is hit from a high position from the rear court on the backhand side of the body. The objective is to hit the shuttle on a high pathway to the back of the opposite court. The stroke can be performed as a defensive clear or an attacking clear by altering the angle of the racket face on impact. This is explained in the forehand overhead clear.

Stand in the ready position with the racket held in the backhand grip. Take the racket back by stepping backwards onto the left foot and twisting the body to the left. Continue the body twist in the shoulders until the back is almost facing the net. The weight is supported on the left foot. The racket arm is flexed, elbow pointing upwards towards the point of impact which is above the right shoulder. To hit the shuttle step across to the left on to the right foot. Throw the racket arm upwards, elbow pointing towards the point of impact. Stop the forward movement of the elbow at the point of impact and allow the rest of the arm to straighten out to bring the racket head through at great speed to hit the shuttle with a strong sudden effort. All the force is concentrated towards the point of impact. After impact the racket arm follows through naturally to drop down and recover.

Practise these stages:

(i) Twist the racket and body to the left and step backwards on the left foot.
(ii) Aim the elbow up towards the point of impact, and step across on the right foot.
(iii) Hold the racket back as long as possible as the throwing action explodes upwards to hit the shuttle at full stretch height.

The feeling of the movement can be experienced by practising without a racket. Simply stand in the ready position, twist the right arm and body to the left as far as it will go. Release the body by flicking upwards with an explosive action. Repeat this several times. Twist slowly to the left and flick upwards suddenly.

Now hold the racket and stand in the ready position. Repeat the practice, this time also stepping across with the right foot to take the body weight as you flick upwards.

23

THE OVERHEAD BACKHAND SMASH (*see* Plate 7)

This stroke is usually played from a mid-court position on the backhand side. The object is to hit the shuttle down quickly and steeply over the net into the opposite court. The preparation for the stroke is identical to the preparation for the overhead backhand clear, except that as in the case of the forehand smash the point of impact is at the side of the body and slightly forwards.

*Preparation:* Stand in the position of readiness and hold the racket in the backhand grip. Take the racket back by stepping backwards with the left foot and twisting the body to the left until the back of the shoulders are almost facing the net. The feet are now sideways to the net with the weight on the left foot. Point the right elbow up towards the point of impact.

*Action:* Throw the arm upwards, elbow leading, with an explosive movement. Allow the arm to straighten out and flick the wrist forwards at speed. At the moment of impact slightly forwards of the body the racket face points downwards to hit the shuttle with great force. The shuttle travels down quickly and steeply.

*Recovery:* Allow the arm to follow through naturally to recover and balance as the force of the stroke dies away.

*Practice:* Prepare for the stroke. Begin the hitting action and try to stop the racket head at the point of impact. Examine your position. The body is stretched upwards, the weight is on the right foot, arm and wrist fully extended and the racket face pointing downwards.

Practise this movement slowly until it can be performed in one continuous movement. Concentrate on a slow gentle preparation, a strong sudden hitting action and a natural follow through of the arm to recover and balance.

THE OVERHEAD BACKHAND DROP SHOT

Drop shots are played on the backhand side for the same reasons as those played on the forehand side.

THE SLOW DROP SHOT

*Preparation:* Stand in the position of readiness. Hold the racket in the backhand grip. Step backwards on to the left foot and twist the body round to the left. Point the right elbow up towards the point of impact. The point of impact is at a position above the right shoulder.

*Action:* Increase the pressure of the grip. Throw the arm upwards with the elbow leading the movement. Allow the body to untwist and stretch upwards as the arm leads the way. The racket head gathers speed as the arm straightens out. Just prior to the impact brake the forward speed of the racket head and continue the movement to hit the shuttle gently. The racket face hits the shuttle slightly upwards and forwards to stroke softly through the shuttle.

*Recovery:* The arm and racket follow through after the shuttle before naturally falling and recovering in a balanced position.

The longer it is possible to delay the braking action of the racket head, the greater the deception in the stroke. The important factor is that the movement does not stop during the hitting phase. The racket head speed slows down abruptly, though the movement is continuous throughout the complete stroke.

The order of movement in the hitting phase is always shoulder, elbow, forearm, wrist, racket head. Practise until the arm can be straightened out in this order with an even flowing movement.

FAST DROP SHOT

The action is identical to the slow drop shot. The difference is that the point of impact is slightly forwards of the body to allow the racket head to hit the shuttle from above, and allow the racket face to direct the shuttle downwards. It is hit downwards with even forward speed to send the shuttle over the net, before it drops to the ground.

THE POINT OF IMPACT ON OVERHEAD STROKES

*Forehand and Backhand Clears* – the point of impact is directly above the body.

*Forehand and Backhand Smash* – impact is slightly forwards of the body.

*Forehand and Backhand Drop Shots*

Slow Drop Shot – above the body.

Fast Drop Shot – forwards of the body.

## 7. THE STROKES—(b) UNDERARM

These are the strokes in which the shuttle is hit from a low position.

THE UNDERARM FOREHAND CLEAR (*see* Plate 8)

This stroke is played from a low position on the forehand side of the body. The shuttle is hit upwards with an underarm action, and directed high and deep to the opposite court.

*Preparation:* Stand in the position of readiness. Hold the racket in the forehand grip. Twist the body to the right and lift the arm back with the wrist cocked, the racket head pointing upwards. The left side of the body points towards the net. Step forwards and across with the left foot. Plant the left foot on the ground to take the body weight. Examine the position. The left side and feet are pointing towards the opposite court. The racket is held back with the arm flexed and the wrist cocked. The racket head is pointing upwards.

*Hitting Action:* The point of impact is in front of the body on the forehand side.

Begin throwing the racket forwards. The wrist leads the movement as the weight transfers to the front foot. The wrist straightens out as the arm extends forwards. The racket head is whipped forward at speed to travel from below the shuttle. The racket face points in the direction forwards and upwards on impact. After impact keep the feet planted and the body low as the arm naturally follows through in the direction of the shuttle.

*Recovery:* The arm continues to travel high as the racket follows the flight of the shuttle and the body straightens up to recover in a balanced position.

THE UNDERARM FOREHAND LOW RETURN (*see* Plate 9)
This stroke is played from a low position on the forehand side. The intention is to hit the shuttle upwards over the net so that it begins to lose height immediately after crossing the net. The preparation for the stroke is identical to the preparation for the underarm clear.

The racket head is thrown downwards and forwards to meet the shuttle from below and directs it forwards and upwards enough to skim the net. The wrist is kept cocked throughout the hitting phase, so keeping the racket head down and the racket face pointing forwards. After impact the racket follows through to about shoulder height.

The shuttle is hit gently with a continuous forward movement of the racket arm and the wrist remains cocked throughout the stroke.

*Practice:* (i) Play a rally with a partner. The task is to hit the shuttle from a low position on the forehand side. Try to hit the shuttle softly and aim at skimming the net.

(ii) Vary this practice by playing low returns to the partner and then ooccasionally with the same action, whip the racket head forwards at great speed to hit the shuttle high to the back of the opposite court. Very little effort is required and these strokes are easy to improve if practised.

UNDERARM BACKHAND CLEAR (*see* Plate 10)
This is a stroke played from a low position on the backhand side of the body. The intention is to return the shuttle high and deep to the rear of the opposite court.

*Preparation:* Stand in the position of readiness. Hold the racket in the backhand grip, racket head held up, arms flexed. Twist the body to the left and take the racket back in preparation for the stroke. Step forwards and across with the right foot. Plant the right foot, with the right knee slightly flexed supporting the body weight. Examine the position. The body is twisted to the left, racket held back, and the right side of the body and feet pointing towards the net.

*Action:* Point the elbow down towards the point of impact, which is

26

forwards and to the left of the body. Throw the right arm downwards towards the shuttle, and hold the racket head back until the last moment. Just prior to impact whip the racket head forward at speed by flicking the wrist forward. The racket head straightens out last in order to flick upwards from underneath the shuttle. The face of the racket is directly in line with the shuttle, and directs it upwards to the rear of the opposite court.

*Recovery:* Allow the racket head to follow through along the pathway of the shuttle and finish high. As the racket completes the follow through, the weight transfers completely to the front foot and the body straightens up to recover.

### THE UNDERARM BACKHAND LOW RETURN (*see* Plate 11)

This is an underarm stroke played from a low position on the backhand side. The intention is to return the shuttle on a low pathway, so that it skims the net and loses height immediately after crossing the net.

*Preparation:* Prepare as for the underarm backhand clear.

*Action:* Begin the throwing action, elbow pointing towards the point of impact. Keep the racket back throughout the stroke by preventing the wrist from straightening out as the arm travels forwards. The racket face hits the shuttle gently forwards and just high enough to cross the net.

*Recovery:* The racket follows through forwards in the direction of the shuttle, until it reaches shoulder height. The weight transfers completely to the front foot as the arm naturally recovers and the body straightens up.

## 8. THE STROKES—(c) DRIVE STROKES

The drive stroke is a stroke played in a situation when the shuttle is to be hit from approximately shoulder height. The situation arises when the shuttle is too low for an overhead stroke and too high for an underarm stroke. The intention is to hit the shuttle at shoulder height level, so that it travels quickly across the net. The drive stroke can be played on the backhand side or on the forehand side. The stroke can be performed from any part of the court, wherever the shuttle is about shoulder height.

### THE FOREHAND DRIVE (*see* Plate 12)

*Preparation:* Stand in the position of readiness. Hold the racket in the forehand grip. Twist the body to the right, support the body weight mainly on the right foot. Take the racket further back and cock the wrist. Step across to the right on to the left foot. Examine the position. The left side of the body points towards the net. The racket is held back with the wrist cocked. The stance is a sideways throwing position.

*Hitting Action:* This is a sideways throwing action to hit the shuttle on impact at a position opposite the body at shoulder height.

27

Keep the wrist cocked and throw out sideways to meet the shuttle. As the arm straightens out, throw the wrist forwards. The racket head travels forward at speed to hit the shuttle. The racket face meets the shuttle and directs it forwards to skim the net.

*Recovery:* The racket follows through forwards in the direction of the shuttle, as the weight of the body transfers completely to the front foot. The arm then naturally recovers at the completion of the follow through.

THE BACKHAND DRIVE (*see* Plate 13)

This is a similar stroke to the forehand drive played from the backhand side of the body.

*Preparation:* Stand in the position of readiness. Hold the racket in the backhand grip. Twist the body to the left and take the racket back. As the racket moves back turn the right thumb inwards towards the body. Continue the twist in the shoulders until the back of the shoulders are almost facing the net. Point the right elbow towards the point of impact which is shoulder height, at the side of the body. Step across to the left on to the right foot.

*Action:* Throw the arm out to the side, with the racket head held back. Allow the body to untwist, and the body weight to travel forwards on to the front foot. As the arm straightens out, bring the wrist forward to whip the racket head forwards at great speed. The racket face hits the shuttle on impact at a point opposite the right shoulder. The shuttle is directed forwards to skim the net and travel into the opposite court.

*Recovery:* The racket follows through in the direction of the shuttle until the strength fades away and the arm naturally recovers at the completion of the stroke.

The arm travels on a pathway parallel to the floor.


## 9. SERVING

The service is the only time during the game when all the players start from a stationary position. The serve is the stroke which initiates the play.

There are four types of service:

(1) The short serve.
(2) The high serve.
(3) The flick serve.
(4) The drive serve.

In the serve the shuttle is hit with an underarm stroke. The shuttle must be below waist height at the moment of impact with the racket, and the racket head must be below the hand of the server. It follows that the shuttle must travel upwards before it crosses the net.

28

## (i) THE SHORT SERVE (*see* Plate 14)

FIG. 3
The object of the short serve is to hit the shuttle from the front of the service court, so that it passes over the net and lands on the front service line of the opposite court.

*Short Serve*
**A** shows serving position.
**X** shows placement of the serve.

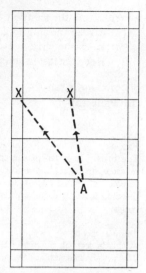

The receiver prepares to attack the short serve, therefore the shuttle must skim the net and begin to lose height immediately on passing over the net. To achieve this requires an accurate, controlled service. If the short serve passes too high above the net the receiver can easily step forwards and hit it down to the ground. A good short serve forces the receiver to hit the shuttle upwards and allows the serving side to gain the attack. The short serve is used mainly in Doubles but can be used with effect in Singles.

*Preparation:* Stand close to the centre service line and about two or three feet from the front service line. Place the left foot forwards until the feet are a comfortable distance apart. The right foot supports most of the body weight.

Hold the racket in the forehand grip. Swing the racket back and cock the wrist. Hold the shuttle by the feathers with a gentle grip of the finger and thumb of the left hand. The aim now is to play an underarm stroke to skim the shuttle over the net.

*Action:* Keep the wrist cocked throughout the stroke.

Swing the racket forward as you release the shuttle by opening the finger and thumb. The racket face meets the shuttle from underneath and gently pushes it over the net.

*Recovery:* The racket arm follows the flight of the shuttle as the body weight travels over the front foot. The racket head keeps low on the follow through so that the racket face points directly towards the pathway of the shuttle.

Practise this movement until it is possible to skim the net and make the shuttle land on the front line of the opposite court. Remember to:

29

(i) Watch the shuttle throughout the stroke.

(ii) Stroke the shuttle gently.

(iii) Keep the wrist cocked.

(iv) Keep the feet in contact with the ground until completion of the stroke.

(ii) THE HIGH SERVE
(*see* Plate 15)

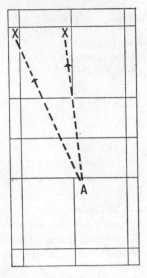

FIG. 4
The intention is to hit the shuttle from the serving position, to travel high and deep to land on the back service line of the opposite court. The shuttle can be directed towards either corner of the opposite service court.

*Doubles Serve*
**A** shows serving position.
**X** shows placement of the serve.

*Preparation:* Stand in the serving position. Prepare as for the short serve, though the racket may be held a little higher on the backswing.

*Action:* Swing the racket down and forwards as the shuttle is released by the finger and thumb of the left hand. Just prior to impact, uncock the wrist and whip the racket head forwards at speed to hit the shuttle from below. The racket face directs the shuttle upwards, high and deep into the opposite service court.

*Recovery:* The racket follows through high in the direction of the shuttle. The arm follows its natural swing up and across the body as the weight transfers fully on to the front foot on the completion of the stroke.

It is not a difficult stroke to perform though it needs practice. It is used as a tactical serve. Hit the shuttle high so that it will drop steeply and become difficult for the receiver to judge the timing of his return stroke. Practise serving high and deep to both corners of the opposite service court.

(iii) THE FLICK SERVE
The flick serve is a surprise serve, used to deceive the opponent. The action is almost identical to the short serve, prior to impact with the shuttle. The intention is to deceive the receiver into thinking he is about to receive a short serve. At the last moment, the shuttle is flicked upwards to pass at a

30

height just above the receiver's reach and then drop quickly into the court.
*Preparation:* Stand in the serving position. Prepare as for the short serve.

*Action:* Swing the racket forwards with the wrist cocked, as the shuttle is released by the left hand. Immediately prior to impact, flick the wrist forwards so that the racket head increases speed to hit the shuttle upwards over the receiver's outstretched reach. The weight travels forwards on to the front foot as the shuttle is hit.

*Recovery:* The wrist continues forward as the racket follows through in the direction of the shuttle. The arm recovers naturally on completion of the stroke.

The later the hitting action can be delayed, the more deceptive is the serve. The serve is a tactical one to make the receiver hesitate in rushing forwards to attack the short serve.

## (iv) THE DRIVE SERVE

The intention is to drive the shuttle at the receiver. The shuttle travels towards the receiver so quickly that he is forced to rush his stroke. It is a surprise serve and used as a tactical move. To comply with the rules of serving, the drive serve must be hit from an underarm position. The shuttle skims the net, and travels quickly upwards. For this reason it should not be used too often. A thoughtful receiver will soon recognise the serve and deal with it easily.

Because the shuttle travels upwards after crossing the net, the server should try to keep the serve as low as possible.

Take up the serving position a pace further back than usual. The action is identical to the short serve. The wrist must remain cocked throughout the stroke, to keep the racket head low and allow the racket face to point forwards. The racket head is kept low on the follow through.

Practise the drive serve in the following way:

(1) Serve a short serve. The racket travels at a slow pace.
(2) Repeat the same action and increase the speed of the swing forward. The shuttle travels faster and continues to rise after crossing the net.
(3) Repeat the same action and increase the speed of the racket arm even more. Do this practice until it is possible to perform a quick movement without allowing the racket head to follow through high.

The drive serve should be aimed at the face of the receiver or at the back-hand side of the receiver. If it is aimed at the forehand side of the receiver it is easy to return. The receiver has only to raise his racket to block the serve, and it loses its effect.

## GENERAL POINTS ABOUT SERVING

As the shuttle is hit upwards in serving, there is a danger that the receiver may gain the attack.

The serve is one of the most important strokes in the game and should be mastered. It is possible to gain the attack with the serve, but to do so requires great accuracy and control.

(1) Watch the shuttlecock. The receiver is usually standing in an aggressive receiving position, ready to attack a poor serve. Do not allow this to distract you from concentrating on serving the shuttle.

(2) Keep both feet in contact with the ground throughout the stroke.

(3) Keep the racket head below the level of the hand holding the racket and hit the shuttle from below waist height.

(4) Decide beforehand what type of serve you intend to do and take your time in making the stroke.

## 10. RECEIVING SERVICE

It is necessary to know how to receive the serve. There are different movements required for receiving each type of serve. The one common factor is the stance taken when preparing to receive the serve. The stance is the starting position prior to any particular serve (*see* Plate 16).

Stand in the forehand court (the right court). Occupy a position about a pace from the centre service line, and one or two feet from the front service line. The left foot is placed forwards so that the feet are a comfortable distance apart, and the body weight is evenly balanced. Flex the knees and lean forwards so that the body weight is supported mainly by the front foot. Hold the racket in front of you in the forehand grip. Keep the head of the racket up and look at the server and the shuttle. This is an alert comfortable position which allows speed of movement forwards or backwards.

PRACTICE

(*a*) Stand in the receiving position and move towards the net as quickly as possible.

(*b*) Stand in the receiving position and move backwards to the rear of the court as quickly as possible.

RECEIVING THE SHORT SERVE

There are three basic replies to the short service. These are as follows.

*The Dab Shot:* The intention of this stroke is to attack the serve. As the shuttle passes over the net, the receiver moves towards the net, reaches forward and taps or dabs the shuttle down towards the ground.

Stand in the receiving position. Step forwards. Reach out towards the net, with the racket head raised and wrist cocked. Dab the wrist forwards with a quick light movement, so that the head of the racket hits the shuttle down towards the ground. The arm reaches forwards and the wrist performs the dabbing action (*as illustrated in* Plate 17). There is no follow through to

32

this stroke. The recovery is a rebound action of the racket after the impact. Practise this movement in the following way. Stand on the front service line facing the net. Reach forwards to the net and make a continuous quick light tapping action of the racket over the top of the net. In this way it is quite easy to experience the rebound after the dabbing action. This stroke is used for all short serves which are high enough to hit downwards.

A variation of this shot is used when the shuttle is just below net height. Using the same action the shuttle is pushed quickly upwards, past the server to land in the half court area. This is called the Push Stroke.

*The Underarm Net Shot:* This stroke is played to return a good short serve, when it is not possible to hit the shuttle down.

Stand in the receiving position. Step forward to attack the shuttle. Stretch the racket forward and drop the racket head quickly to meet the shuttle from below. The racket face meets the shuttle as near the top of the net as possible. A gentle upward movement of the outstretched racket will stroke the shuttle back over the net for it to drop down the other side. The aim is to hit the shuttle so that it almost creeps over the net (*see* Plate 18).

*Underarm High Clear:* If the shuttle has dropped too low for it to be returned from net height, an alternative stroke is the underarm clear, high and deep to the rear of the court. This stroke is played with the same action as the normal underarm clear. However, as the receiving stance is such that the racket head is held up in front of the body, there is no time for a full backswing as the shuttle comes over the net.

Stand in the receiving position. Step forwards to attack the serve. As the shuttle falls, drop the racket head below the pathway of the shuttle. Cock the wrist quickly and flick the racket head up at speed to hit the shuttle high and deep into the opposite court. The racket travels up to follow through in the direction of the shuttle before the arm naturally recovers. At the completion of the stroke the body straightens up to recover in a balanced position.

RECEIVING THE HIGH SERVE

Stand in the receiving position. As the shuttle is served high and deep to the back of the court, you must push off the front foot to travel quickly to the back of the court.

Move quickly backwards to get behind the shuttle. Stop and balance as you prepare to hit the shuttle. The situation is now similar to any overhead stroke. The emphasis is on reacting quickly to the serve to get into a hitting position. Once in position any overhead stroke can be played. The usual reply in Doubles play to a high serve is to play an overhead forehand smash. So smash straight or to the centre.

To move quickly to the rear of the court from the receiving position requires good footwork and balance. It is possible to move backwards, with either a side skipping action or a running action.

The preparation for the stroke can be made whilst travelling to the rear of the court or on arrival at the rear of the court. The choice is a personal one but will be made naturally according to the time available in the situation.

RECEIVING THE FLICK SERVE
Stand in the receiving position. The server appears to be serving a short serve, you are ready to move forwards. At the last moment, the shuttle is flicked upwards above your outstretched reach. It now requires speed of movement to move backwards to reach the shuttle before it drops to the ground.

Move quickly backwards into a position that you can smash the shuttle down from an overhead position.

It is not always possible to place the feet behind the shuttle, though it is possible to place the racket behind the shuttle by bending backwards, or jumping back even though off balance.

Only practice and experience will enable you to manipulate your body in this way. If the smash is not possible, an alternative stroke can be played, i.e. the overhead forehand clear or the overhead forehand drop shot. When you have been deceived by the serve and find yourself in an awkward position, whatever you do, make sure you return the shuttle back over the net.

RECEIVING THE DRIVE SERVE
The shuttle approaches at speed on a rising pathway. Stand in the receiving position. Hold the racket in the forehand grip with the racket head held up. Remember the instructions for the drive serve. To perform a good drive serve it is necessary to stand further back in the court; if you see the server do this, then you can anticipate the serve and be ready for it.

As the shuttle approaches at speed the immediate reaction is to make a hurried smashing action. There is not enough time to do this.

(a) Raise the racket head higher, to place the face of the racket in line with the oncoming shuttle, cock the wrist and tap the shuttle lightly back over the net down to the ground.

(b) Raise the racket head higher in line with the shuttle – block the shot. The shuttle bounces off the racket and drops over the net.

(c) Raise the racket head higher, racket face in line with the shuttle, and tap the shuttle upwards, high and deep to the rear of the opposite court.

These actions can be performed when the shuttle is driven towards the forehand side or the backhand side. If the shuttle arrives on the backhand side move the racket across the front of the body to play a forehand stroke from the backhand side of the body.

Practise this movement: Stand in the receiving position, move the right

34

arm across the front of the body with the forehand face pointing towards the net. Practise tapping down, tapping up and blocking.

## 11. NET PLAY

Net Play takes place in the area between the front service line and the net. There are a limited number of possible shots in the situations which develop in this area. It is necessary to become familiar with the strokes possible in the situations created.

A player at the net has two objectives. The first objective is to hit an outright winner. The second objective is to force the opponent to play a defensive stroke or make an error.

To achieve the first objective the player must create a situation which allows him to hit the shuttle down to the ground for a winning shot. To achieve the second objective a stroke is played which forces the opponent to hit the shuttle upwards.

Stand in the position of readiness. Occupy a position on the centre of the front service line facing the net, keep alert, concentrate and watch the shuttle and always keep the racket head up.

(1) If the shuttle is above the height of the net, place the racket head in line with the oncoming shuttle and either tap it or push it down towards the ground.

(2) If the shuttle is below net height, play the stroke as early as possible, i.e. meet it near the top of the net. Place the racket head in line with the oncoming shuttle. The racket face meets the shuttle from below and gently strokes it upwards over the net so that it passes close to the top of the net and falls steeply to the ground, immediately after crossing the net.

(3) If the shuttle has fallen near the ground before you play the stroke either return a low net shot away from your opponent or flick it past him so that it falls behind him in the mid-court area.

The basic strokes for net play are dab shots and underarm strokes. These are described in detail in 'Receiving the Short Serve' (page 36). One other stroke is the block stroke; when the shuttle is travelling at speed across the net, time does not allow a dab stroke or an underarm stroke to be performed. As with receiving the drive serve, the best tactic is to block the shuttle by placing the racket face directly in line with the pathway of the oncoming shuttle, the shuttle bounces off the racket and drops down over the net.

The essentials of Net Play are:

(a) An alert ready position.

(b) Watch the shuttle.

(c) Keep the racket head up.

(d) Hold the racket with a gentle grip of the fingers.

35

(e) Basic shots are dab stroke, underarm stroke, block stroke.

(f) Play net shots at a comfortable distance from the shuttle, usually at arms length.

## 12. FOOTWORK, BALANCE AND STROKE PLAY

Good control of the body is necessary to play Badminton. To play any stroke in the game situation involves a sequence of movements. From a fixed position, the player must move into a hitting position, play the stroke and move to the next position. This requires travelling on the feet to move into the hitting position. On arrival in the hitting position the player must stop and balance. The feet support the body in the balance position. Balance is essential to allow the player to perform the movements of the upper body required to hit the shuttle. The movements of the upper body are: a preparation for the stroke, the hitting action and a recovery from the action. Unnecessary movements of the feet during the hitting action can upset the rhythm of the stroke and effect accuracy and control. The sequence of movement for any stroke in any situation is: travel, balance, prepare, hit, recover. This should take place as one continuous movement.

### (i) TRAVEL

The player travels on his feet from one position to another, and movements of the feet should be quick and light. Practise in the following ways. Begin in the centre of the court from the ready position:

(a) Run with quick light movements of the feet in the directions forwards and backwards.

(b) skip sideways to the front of the court and to the back of the court. Do this facing the right side of the court and repeat the action whilst facing the left side of the court.

(c) Practise running, and change to skipping sideways in different directions.

(d) Practise skipping sideways and change to running in different directions.

### (ii) BALANCE

Balance is essential during the hitting phase. The feet are still in the balanced position.

(a) Practise running and skipping forwards and backwards, and stop suddenly to balance.

(b) Practise travelling in different directions on the court and stop suddenly to balance.

### (iii) PREPARATION, ACTION AND RECOVERY

Preparation is the movement which takes the racket in the backswing ready to hit forwards into the shuttle.

The action is the hitting movement.

The recovery is the natural movement of the racket arm after the hitting movement.

(a) *Practice:* Select a stroke. Prepare with a light effort. Hit forwards with a strong sudden movement. Recover naturally, i.e. as the force of the stroke dies away, allow the racket arm to continue easily on its natural pathway until completion of the stroke.

Repeat this practice with the selected stroke. Perform the movements separately and then try to join them together to make one continuous movement.

(b) *Practice:* Stand in the ready position in the centre of the court. Select a stroke to practise and decide on the position you will play it from. Now try to join all the movements together to make a continuous, flowing pattern of movement.

From the ready position, travel, balance, prepare, hit, recover and return to your starting position.

The ability to perform these basic actions in a continuous sequence of movement, will help to raise the performance of your game.


## 13. SIMPLE PRACTICES FOR THE STROKES

Stroke practice plays an important part in improving stroke production. It is not always possible to improve strokes during a game. In a game, the atmosphere is competitive and the intention is to win the game. A learner does not have time to think about performing the correct stroke, and he has not yet reached the stage when the correct stroke is an automatic action. During a game it is usually satisfactory if a learner can return the shuttle back into play without having to think about footwork, balance and correct stroke production. Only time and playing experience will enable the learner to play the correct stroke in the game situation.

It is important that the learner practises the strokes in a situation which is not competitive. Instead the learner should practise the strokes with a friend. It will not matter if mistakes are made, for the intention of a practice session is to allow mistakes and concentrate on eliminating them gradually to acquire perfect stroke production. The aim of practice is 'to groove the stroke'; that is, to repeat the same stroke continuously, and so make the movements automatic.

The following practices are a few simple ones to begin with.

HOW TO PRACTISE STROKES

The ideal situation is to play on a singles court with a partner. This is not

37

always possible in a club because other players are waiting to play. The Doubles game is played most in a Badminton Club to provide an opportunity for more players to play at one time. However, it is customary to allow a short period for a 'knock up', in which the players loosen up. Use this 'knock up' period wisely to practise selected strokes. If this is done on each occasion in the 'knock up' period, the strokes will eventually improve. For this reason the following practices are designed for the 'knock up' period. If you ever have the opportunity to practise on the full court for any length of time, then make the most of it.

# OVERHEAD STROKE PRACTICES
## OVERHEAD FOREHAND CLEAR

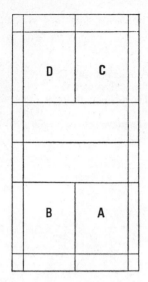

FIG. 5
**A** and **B** 'knock up' with **C** and **D** before the game begins.
**A** practises with **C**.
**B** practises with **D**.
The following instructions for **A** and **C** also apply to **B** and **D**.

The players stand in the positions as shown on the diagram.

Both players begin from the mid-court area.
**A** serves high to **C**.

**C** plays a forehand clear to **A** and **A** returns the shuttle with an overhead forehand clear. This continuous play is called a rally. Both players begin from the mid-court area practising overhead forehand clears. By hitting the shuttle higher and deeper each time they try to work their way to the rear of the court. The intention of this practice is to try to hit the shuttle with an overhead forehand clear, from one end of the court to the other.

Count the number of shots exchanged before the rally breaks down. By trying to improve on the score each time the players will be able to record their progress. A few minutes like this at the beginning of each game will help to improve personal performance in correct stroke production.

## OVERHEAD BACKHAND CLEAR
Repeat the above practice using overhead backhand clears. This may be difficult at first as it is not easy to return the shuttle accurately to the backhand side of your partner. If it is necessary to play the occasional overhead forehand clear to keep the rally going then do so. However, as the practice is a backhand practice, make every effort to use the backhand stroke whenever possible. With continual practice in this way, it will not be long before you can perform overhead backhand clears continually.

FIG. 6
**A** practises with **C**.
**B** practises with **D**.
The instructions for **A** and **C** also apply to **B** and **D**.

The players stand in the positions as shown on the diagram.

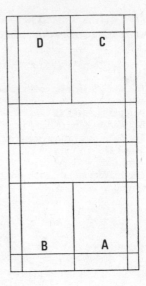

(1) **C** serves a high serve to **A**.
(2) **A** smashes the shuttle back to land in front of **C**.
(3) If **C** can return the shuttle with an underarm clear he does so. If **C** cannot return the smash he begins again with another high serve to **A**.
(4) After 5–10 smashes the players change over for **A** to serve to **C**.

OVERHEAD BACKHAND SMASH
Repeat the above practice but use the overhead backhand smash.

OVERHEAD SLOW DROP SHOT AND UNDERARM
CLEAR

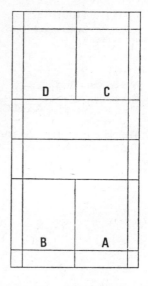

FIG. 7
(a) Both strokes are played on the forehand side.
**A** practises with **C**.
**B** practises with **D**.
The instructions for **A** and **C** also apply to **B** and **D**.

The players stand in the positions as shown on the diagram.

(1) **C** serves high to **A**.
(2) **A** plays an overhead forehand slow drop shot. He aims the shuttle to land between the net and the front service line.
(3) **C** steps forward and returns the shuttle to **A** by playing an underarm forehand clear.
(4) After 5–10 drop shots from **A** the players change over for **A** to serve to **C**.

(b) Both strokes are played on the backhand side.
Practise as for the overhead forehand drop shot and underarm forehand clear, but hit the shuttle with backhand strokes.

OVERHEAD FAST DROP SHOT AND UNDERARM CLEAR
Repeat the practice as for the slow drop shot. In this case the player feeding the shuttle for his partner to practise should step back to the mid-court area. The fast shot will skim the net and travel into the court beyond the front service line. The feeder moves back into a position to return the shuttle.

Practise the fast drop shot and underarm clear on the forehand side and the backhand side.

## DRIVE STROKES
### FOREHAND AND BACKHAND DRIVES

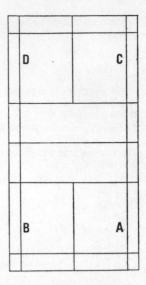

FIG. 8
A practises with C.
B practises with D.
The instructions for A and C apply also to B and D.

The players stand in the positions as shown in the diagram, i.e. near the side lines.

(1) C serves a drive serve down the line, to the forehand side of A.
(2) A plays a forehand drive. The shuttle is driven from shoulder height to skim the net and travel to the backhand side of C.
(3) C plays a backhand drive to return the shuttle back to the forehand side of A.
(4) The players attempt a rally of 10 shots.
(5) The players change over for A to practise backhand drives and C to practise forehand drives.

## UNDERARM STROKES
FOREHAND AND BACKHAND UNDERARM LOW
RETURNS

FIG. 9
**A** practises with **C**.
**B** practises with **D**.
The instructions for **A** and **C** also apply to **B** and **D**.

The players stand in the positions as shown in the diagram.

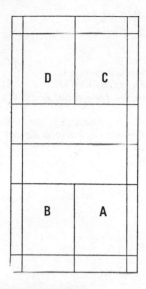

All low returns should skim the net and land about mid-court.
(1) **C** plays a low serve to **A**
(2) **A** plays an underarm forehand low return to **C**
(3) **C** plays an underarm backhand low return to **A**.
(4) The players play a rally of 10 shots and then change over.
(5) **C** plays underarm forehand low returns. **A** plays underarm backhand low returns.
(6) Both players practise underarm low returns from either the forehand side or the backhand side. Play a rally of 20 shots.

Fig. 10
A practises with C.
B practises with D.
The instructions for A and C also apply to B and D.

The players stand in the positions as shown in the diagram, i.e. between the net and the front service line.

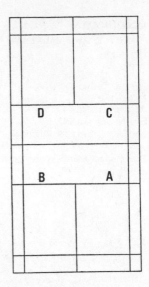

The aim of this practice is to improve net strokes. Requirements are good balance, a gentle touch and control of the racket face. The players try to hit the shuttle so that it keeps very low when passing over the net. The shuttle should travel to land between the front service line and the net. A good net shot is when the shuttle drops very close to the net. Try to hit the shuttle from a position at the top of the net whenever possible.

(1) C throws the shuttle over the net to A.
(2) A hits the shuttle back to C and a rally commences.
(3) If the rally breaks down, C begins it again by throwing the shuttle over the net to A.


SERVING
It has been explained earlier that the service is the only time in the game when all the players begin from a stationary position. For this reason a player has time to think about performing the correct action in a game. When serving during a game, take your time, concentrate on performing the correct action and the stroke will eventually improve. If you wish to improve the serve further, the following practices are useful.

THE SHORT SERVE

FIG. 11
A practises with C.
B practises with D.
The instructions for A and C also apply to B and D.

The players stand in the positions as shown in the diagram.

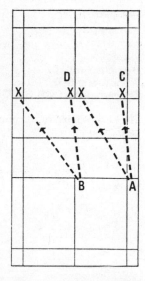

X shows where the shuttle should land. In the short serve, the shuttle should be aimed to land on the front service line, either at the centre or the side of the service court.

(1) A serves a low serve to C.
(2) C allows the shuttle to land. A can then judge the accuracy of his serve.
(3) C picks up the shuttle and throws it back to A.
(4) A serves again.
(5) After 5–10 serves, the players change over and C practises the short serve.

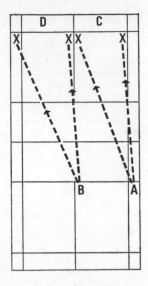

FIG. 12
A practises with C.
B practises with D.
The instructions for A and C also apply to B and D.

The players stand in the positions as shown in the diagram.

X shows where the shuttle should land. In the high serve the shuttle should be aimed to land at the centre or the side of the back service line.

(1) A serves a high serve to either the centre or the side of the opposite service court.
(2) C allows the shuttle to land. A can judge the accuracy of the serve.
(3) C picks up the shuttle and returns it to A.
(4) A repeats the high serve.
(5) After 5–10 serves the players change over and C practises the high serve.

FLICK SERVES AND DRIVE SERVES
Both of these serves are surprise serves. At this stage the short serve and the high serve should be mastered by practice. The flick serve and the drive serve can be practised in the game situation when the element of surprise is most required.

14. BASIC TACTICS
The aim of a contest is to win. To win it is necessary to hit the shuttle to the ground in the opposite court. At the same time you must prevent the shuttle reaching the ground on your court. The ability to perform the basic strokes allows you to achieve these ends. A knowledge of tactics gives you greater opportunity to play the strokes.

Tactics mean the art of manoeuvring. In Badminton this involves manoeuvring yourself and your opponent into positions which allow you to defend your own court and attack your opponents' court.

When your opponent hits the shuttle you must stand in the best possible position on the court to reach all his shots. When you hit the shuttle, you must know where to hit it to make the best possible advantage of the situation.

Certain basic tactics have evolved because of:

(1) The size of the court.
(2) The height of the net.
(3) The varying flight of the shuttle.
(4) The type of game, i.e. the Singles or Doubles.

*These factors are constant. There is no one correct tactic in any one particular situation, but the following may be a basis from which to begin.*

## THE SINGLES GAME

The Singles Court is long and narrow. The emphasis is on the players moving forwards and backwards rather than side to side. The most common strokes are clears and drop shots. The idea is to move the opponent out of position:

(*a*) to the back of the court with clears;
(*b*) towards the net, with drop shots.

These can be varied by altering the speed of the shuttle. The smash can be used effectively to attack a weak return or to speed up the play and force the opponent into making an error.

SINGLES TACTICS

(1) *Central Base:* Occupy a position which is approximately in the centre of the court. This position is an equal distance from any area of the court. It enables you to defend the whole court against all possible shots and to move quickly into position to play a stroke. This base can be adjusted slightly from one side of the court to the other. It is adjusted in relation to the possible angle of return of the shuttle. If the opponent is about to hit the shuttle from the forehand corner of the rear court, the base will move slightly to the left to narrow the angle of return. If the opponent hits the shuttle from his backhand corner the base will move slightly to the right of the centre to narrow the angle of return.

47

Fig. 13

Possible direction of shuttle flight:

Line bisecting angle of return:

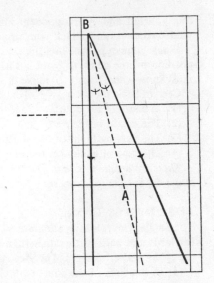

**B** plays stroke from forehand corner.

**A** moves his base slightly to the left of the centre service line to narrow the angle of return.

(2) *Return to the Central Base:* After hitting the shuttle from any position on court, return to the central base as quickly as possible.

(3) *Moving the Opponent:* Try to move your opponent away from his central base. If he can be moved out of position, more of the court is left open for a return stroke, and an opening is created for a winning shot.

(4) *How to move the Opponent:* The most common strokes are clears to the back of the court and drop shots close to the net. Hit the shuttle to the open spaces and make your opponent run the full distance of the court, i.e. a simple sequence of shots could be as follows:

Clear to the forehand corner, drop shot to the backhand net corner, clear to the backhand corner, clear to the forehand corner, drop shot to the backhand net corner.

By keeping the opponent on the move and stretching him the full distance of the court each time he will become fatigued, slow in recovering to his centre and eventually make a poor return to enable you to hit a winning shot.

(5) *Playing the Correct Stroke:* The ability to move the opponent around the court away from his central base, presupposes that you can play all the strokes. Practise the strokes. Aim drop shots close to the net, and play clears high and deep to the baseline. Use the smash from the mid-court whenever possible and smash to the nearest open space, or down the sideline.

(6) *Serving:* Serve high and deep to the rear of the court. You are already

PLATE 1. Position of Readiness. (*Left*) Face view. (*Right*) Side view

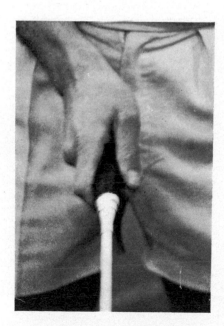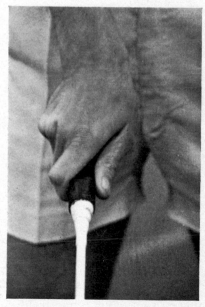

PLATE 2. Forehand grip                    PLATE 3. Backhand grip

PLATE 4. Movement progression in overhead forehand clear. (*Left*) Preparation for stroke. (*Right*) Completion of stroke

PLATE 5. Overhead forehand smash. (*Left*) Preparation. (*Centre*) Action. (*Right*) Recovery

PLATE 6. Overhead backhand clear. (*Left*) Preparation. (*Right*)
Point of impact

PLATE 7. Overhead backhand smash. (*Left*) Preparation. (*Right*)
The smash

PLATE 8. Underarm forehand clear. (*Left*) Preparation. (*Right*) Completion of stroke

PLATE 9. Underarm forehand low return. (*Left*) Preparation. (*Above*) Completion of stroke

PLATE 10. Underarm backhand clear. (*Left*) Preparation. (*Right*) Completion of stroke

PLATE 11. Underarm backhand low return. (*Left*) Preparation. (*Above*) Completion of stroke

PLATE 12. Forehand drive. (*Left*) Preparation. (*Right*) Completion of stroke

PLATE 13. Backhand drive (*Left*) Preparation. (*Above*) Completion of stroke

PLATE 14. The short serve. (*Left*) Preparation. (*Right*)
The serve

PLATE 15. The high serve. (*Left*) Preparation. (*Right*)
Completion of serve

PLATE 16. Receiving service. (*Left*) Front view. (*Right*)
Side view

PLATE 17. The dab shot. (*Left*) Preparation. (*Right*) Completion
of stroke

PLATE 18. Underarm net shot. (*Left*) Forehand net shot. (*Right*)
Backhand net shot

in the central position, balanced and ready. Your opponent now has to move away from his central base. Only serve short if the opponent is standing so far back that he cannot attack the short serve.

(7) *Receiving Service:* Stand in a position about a pace behind the front service line. If the serve is high, move quickly back and play the first return as an overhead clear. Do this to move the server away from his central base. Return the serve and move quickly to your central base.

(8) *Playing the Stroke:* Always move to meet the shuttle. Do not wait for it to arrive. The earlier you can hit the shuttle, the less time you give your opponent to return to his centre.

The above tactics and advice are based on an appreciation of several constant factors. There are other factors which may be considered in adopting tactics. With more experience it is possible to consider the relative strength and weakness of an opponent with regard to:

*Ability to perform strokes:* If the opponent is weak on the backhand strokes it would be sound policy to hit the shuttle to the backhand side. A weak return from the backhand presents the opportunity for an attacking shot. Learn to recognise weaknesses and exploit them.

*Fitness:* Fitness is of paramount importance in singles. An unfit opponent will become fatigued quickly and make errors in stroke production. Prolong the rallies and keep the opponent on the move.

*Speed in Moving:* A slow mover tends to be slow in reaching the shuttle and returning to the centre. Speed up the game by playing attacking overhead clears and fast drop shots. Do not allow your opponent time to reach the shuttle or time to recover after playing a stroke.

These are a few additional factors which may help you to decide what tactics to adopt. With experience they can be an invaluable assistance towards winning.

# SINGLES TACTICS. DEVELOPMENT
## SERVICE AND RECEIVING SERVICE

FIG. 14
Shows pathway of shuttle in serve:

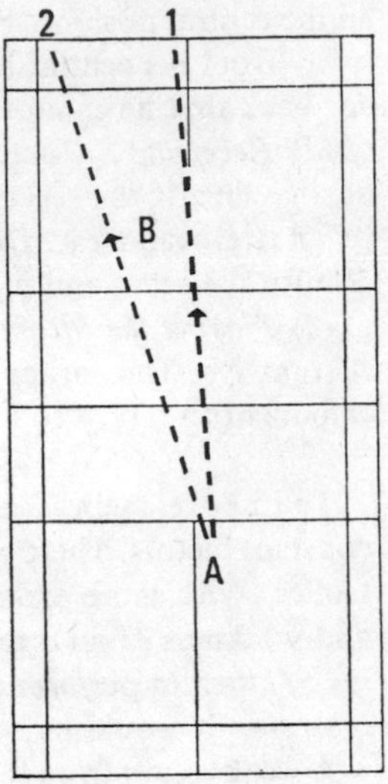

To commence the game the players stand in the positions as shown.

**A** serves high to **B** and directs the shuttle towards the centre (1) or the corner (2). The shuttle is served high to drop vertically on the rear service line. The serve forces **B** to move away from the centre to hit the shuttle.

**B** stands mid-court but nearer the front. He must prepare for a short serve and cannot stand too far back in the court. If the serve is high **B** has time to move back as the shuttle will take time to travel the full distance of the court.

FIG. 15
An example of positional play based on the possible
angle of return is shown by **A** the server.

Serve:

Possible return of serve:

Line dividing angle of return:

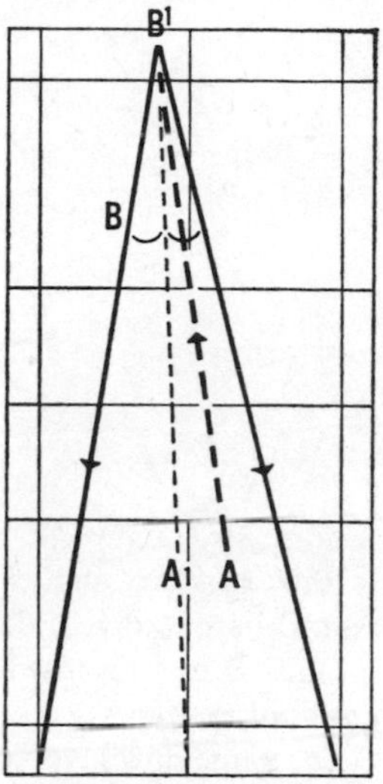

(1) **A** serves high to **B** and directs the shuttle to the position as shown.

(2) **B** moves back to **BI** to hit the shuttle.

(3) **B** can return the shuttle to the forehand or backhand corner of the
opposite court.

(4) **A** considers this possibility and places himself directly between the
angle of possible returns, i.e. **A** moves to **AI**, which is to the left of his
serving position.

If **A** serves to the forehand corner of the opposite service court **A** will
move his base even further to the left. *See* Fig. 16.

51

FIG. 16

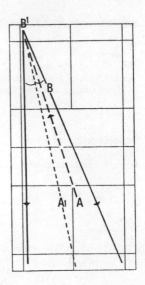

With practice and experience it becomes possible to adopt a suitable central base to divide the angle of return for any shot.

Once **B** has returned the serve the game opens up. The players are in constant motion.

The game now involves each player trying to manoeuvre the other around the court by using a variety of strokes, changes of pace of the shuttle speed and deception.

## THE DOUBLES GAME

In Doubles play the emphasis in on attack. The aim of both sides is to try to create an attacking situation. This is achieved by correct use of the strokes and good positional play. The Doubles game is one of continual attack and defence, first by one side and then by the other. Before a side can attack they must create a situation in which the shuttle is in a position to be hit downwards.

A Doubles pair requires knowledge of:

(1) *Attack:*

    (*a*) How to create an attacking situation.

    (*b*) How to make the best possible attack in this situation.

(2) *Defence:*

    (*a*) How to defend against an attack.

    (*b*) How to turn the defence into attack.

Simple if the shuttle can be hit downwards by one side, that side is on the attack. It follows that the opposing side is on the defence.

To create an attacking situation, one side must force the opposing side to hit the shuttle upwards.

There are two basic positional formations in the Doubles game.

(1) The Attacking Formation – the positions the players move into for attack.

(2) The Defensive Formation – the positions the players move into for defence.

These formations will be explained in the following development of a Doubles game. The diagrams are arranged in logical sequence. The sequence explains a normal development of a game, beginning with the serve. Basic doubles tactics are discussed as each diagram is explained. The learner will gain an idea of basic tactics.

The serve is the start of play in Badminton. After each point the players begin from a stationary position until the next serve has been played. All development originates from the serve. The following tactics will be discussed from the beginning.

# DOUBLES TACTICS

STAGE 1. DEVELOPMENT BASED ON A SHORT
SERVE

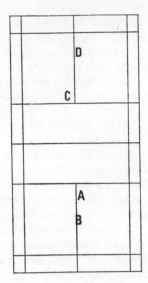

FIG. 17
A and B play against C and D.
Side A and B serve.
Side C and D receive.

The players stand in the positions as shown in the
diagram.

A serves a short serve to C. A aims the shuttle to land on the front service
line.

A moves forwards towards the net with his racket head held up to be in a
position to hit down any low return. He moves only after completion of the
serve.

B stands directly behind A. B is in a position to smash any high return of
serve or reach any low return which goes past A.

C is the receiver. He stands well up to the front service line. His intention
is to attack the shuttle as it comes across the net.

C plays a dab shot downwards past A and directed towards the mid-court
area. C tries to play a net stroke which will force A or B to hit the shuttle
upwards.

D stands nearer the back of the court next to the central line. His task is
to cover the rear court as his partner attacks the serve. D is ready for any
possible high return which passes C.

Each player is ready to perform his task.

The following development is a normal one in Doubles and emphasises
the basic attacking and defensive formations.

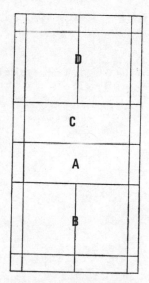

FIG. 18
The players stand in the positions shown in Fig. 18 after the short serve and the receiver's return of serve.

A has played a short serve and followed his serve in to the net. The position is shown in Fig. 18.

C has moved forward to attack the serve and push the shuttle past A into the forehand court. C stays at the net in the position shown in Fig. 18.

B is in the centre ready to move to the shuttle.

D moves forward to the mid-court. waiting to smash a possible weak return from B.

A remains at the net in case his partner B plays a low return. If B does play a low return A must guard the net area.

At this stage of the game only two shots have been played, i.e. the serve and the return of the serve. The players have moved into positions and each side is waiting for the opportunity to seize the attack. The game is at stalemate. If B can now play another low return past the net man C it will remain at stalemate until one player hits the shuttle upwards.

This is a typical situation in a game, with both sides hitting the shuttle low over the net, to the middle of the court. Usually with players at the learner stage, the stroke played after the return of service is a high clear and the game opens up as follows.

FIG. 19
A and B are in a side by side formation.
C and D are in a front and back formation.

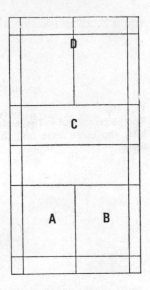

The game develops from stage 2. After C has attacked the serve and hit the shuttle past A, B moves and hits the shuttle high to the opposite court. The players move into the positions as shown above. D moves back into position to hit the shuttle. His aim is to play an overhead forehand smash.

C remains at the net ready to attack a weak return from D's smash. C and D have gained the attack. The attacking formation is called the 'front and back' formation.

C commands the net area and D commands the rear of the court.

A and B have taken up defensive positions which are called the 'sides' formation. Each player is responsible for one side of the court, i.e. from the front to the back of the court. To achieve this formation A has moved back from the net to defend a half of the court. B has moved to the side to defend the other half court.

There are two basic formations in Doubles.

A simple rule to follow in deciding what type of formation to take up is: If the shuttle is high on the opponent's side of the court, immediately take up a 'sides' formation. If the shuttle is high on your side of the court, immediately take up a 'front and back' formation.

FIG. 20
(a) *Defending against a smash from the forehand side.*

Signifies possible direction of smash:

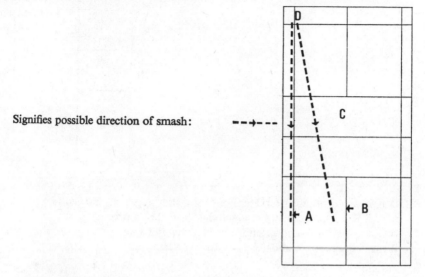

D is in position for an overhead forehand smash. He should smash straight down the line or to the centre.

A and B defend against the possible shots and position themselves accordingly.

A faces the side of the court.

B faces the centre.

Both A and B defend on the backhand side.

FIG. 21
(b) *Defending against a smash from the centre.*

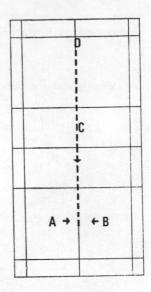

D is in a central position. He should smash straight, to the centre.
A and B defend against a straight smash to the centre.
A faces the centre and defends on the forehand side.
B faces the centre and defends on the backhand side.

FIG. 22
(c) *Defending against a smash from the backhand corner.*

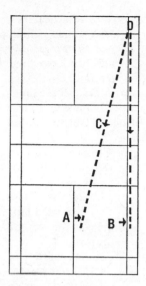

**D** is in position for an overhead smash. **D** should smash straight down the line or to the centre.

**A** and **B** defend against the possible shots and position themselves accordingly.

**B** faces the side of the court.

**A** faces the centre of the court.

Both **A** and **B** defend on the forehand side.

From this simple progression based on the short serve and the reply to the short serve it is possible to establish a few basic factors about Doubles tactics:

(1) *Server:* Serve short and move into the net after serving. A short serve performed accurately is the only serve which gives the best possible chance of forcing the receiver to hit upwards.

(2) *Receiver:* Attack the short serve and try to meet the shuttle as it crosses the net. Unless you do this you will be forced to hit the shuttle upwards and give the serving side a chance to attack.

(3) *Attack:* (a) *Positions.* Whenever the shuttle is returned high to your side of the court you are placed in an attacking situation. The player who can reach the shuttle most easily, moves to play the smash. His partner immediately moves towards the net.

(b) *The Striker.* The player who moves to hit the shuttle from the overhead position has a variety of possible shots. He can smash or play a drop shot. Smash straight or to the centre. Play a drop shot as a

59

surprise tactical shot, to force a weak return and create the opportunity for a winning smash on the next shot.

(c) *The Net Player.* Move into the centre of the net area as quickly as possible. Keep your racket head up and be ready to attack any weak return.

(4) *Defence:* Take up the defensive 'sides' formation if either you or your partner hit the shuttle high to the opposite court. Once in the 'sides' formation, defend on that side of your body, which you expect the straight smash to arrive.

The Objectives of Defence are:

(a) *Defend against the attack.* Defend against a smash by hitting the shuttle high and deep to the rear of the opposite court. Try to alternate the return, and hit the shuttle to the different corners of the court. This keeps the striker on the move. High and deep clears make it difficult for the striker to penetrate your defence. Defend against a drop shot by returning the shuttle high and deep to the rear of the opposite court.

(b) *Defence into the Attack:* Try to turn the defence into attack. If possible, return the smash, so that you hit the shuttle low over the net, past the net player. The shuttle is directed low, towards the middle of the court. The opponent behind the net player must move forward and play an underarm low return or an underarm clear. If the shuttle is returned high to your side immediately take up a 'front and back' attacking formation.

GENERAL SUMMARY

(1) Use the overhead forehand smash to hit the shuttle for the outright winner. Smash whenever possible, and smash straight or to the centre.

(2) Only clear the shuttle high from an overhead position, when you are caught out of position and are unable to play a smash or a drop shot.

(3) Use overhead drop shots as a tactical shot to move your opponent out of position and force a weak return.

(4) Drive Strokes. If the shuttle is too low to smash, meet it early and play a drive stroke. Drive straight or to the centre.

(5) Underarm strokes are used to clear the shuttle high and deep or to hit low returns and force the opponents to hit upwards.

(6) *Varying the Serve.* High serves, flick serves and drive serves are all hit upwards. The receiving side are placed in an attacking situation and take up a front and back formation. The serving side moves into a 'Sides' defensive formation.

THE MIXED DOUBLES GAME

It is assumed that the lady is the weaker player. If the usual Doubles forma-

60

tion is used, this weakness would be exploited by the opposing man. For this reason the mixed doubles game is based on the front and back formation, i.e. the attacking formation. In this way the weaker physique of the lady is not exploited.

In Mixed Doubles the lady controls the forecourt (the net area) and the man controls the remainder of the court. As this is the established formation for play it is vital that each side must gain the attack – and maintain it.

(1) ROLE OF THE LADY
   (a) Stand in the centre of the forecourt, in the ready position with the racket head held up.
   (b) Control the net and attack all low returns.
   (c) Hit the shuttle down for a winner whenever possible, with a dab stroke.
   (d) If unable to hit the shuttle down, play a low return close to the net or to the mid-court area. Force the opposition to hit upwards.
   (e) Be prepared to anticipate a cross court shot from either a drive or a low return and either play a dab shot or block the shuttle so that it drops over the net and forces the opposition to hit upwards.
   (f) Do not hit the shuttle if the point of impact is behind you. Leave it for your partner.

(2) ROLE OF THE MAN
   (a) Stand in the middle of the court behind the lady. Take up the position of readiness and keep the racket head up at all times. Keep behind the lady whenever possible.
   (b) Cover the lady when she attempts to hit a shuttle which has been aimed at the mid-court area, in case she cannot hit it and she allows it to pass her.
   (c) Smash whenever possible.
   (d) Hit upwards as little as possible.
   (e) Aim shots towards the half court area or to the four corners of the court.

Throughout the game much of the play involves low shots to the mid-court area. This is the area between the lady at the net, and the man at the rear. Each side directs the shuttle to this area which is the weak point in the front and back formation. The aim is to manoeuvre the opponents out of position or force them to hit the shuttle upwards.

If the man stands mid-court with his racket head up, he can step across and play a drive stroke to a shuttle arriving in the mid-court area. The drive should be to the opposite mid-court area or deep to the rear of the court to manoeuvre the opposite man out of position. The aim is to force a weak return or create an opening for a winning shot.

*The Short Serve:* The serve should be short and aimed towards the centre.

61

Whoever serves the shuttle, it is still the lady's task to play all net shots.

*The High Serve:* The shuttle is usually only served to the lady to move her away from the net. Whatever type of return the lady makes, she must immediately move quickly back to the net.

A high serve to the man immediately places the man on the attack. Only use the high serve to the man, as a tactical serve.

## 15. UNORTHODOX STROKES

The strokes so far discussed have been orthodox strokes. That is to say that each stroke has involved the most effective and economical movement required to hit the shuttle with the best results. The opportunity to play such a stroke is dependent on the ability of the player to be in the correct position to hit the shuttle. Every player tries to be in the correct position but often even the best players are caught out of position. Even so the shuttle has to be returned over the net into play. To hit the shuttle the player has to improvise a movement and an unorthodox stroke is the result. This type of stroke is not as difficult as it appears, if the underlying principles of stroke play are understood. Fortunately the human body can bend, twist, stretch and arrange itself in various contorted positions. The ability of the body to function in this way allows a player to perform many unorthodox strokes.

The underlying principles of stroke play are as follows:

(1) *Balance.* The body must be in a state of balance to play any type of stroke.

(2) *Movement of the body.* The position of the body must be adjusted to allow the freedom of movement of the racket. This is possible because of the flexibility of the body.

(3) *Control of the racket face.* The racket face must be placed in line with the pathway of the shuttle to enable the shuttle to be directed over the net.

(4) *Awareness of position.* The player must be aware of his position in relation to the opposite court. This awareness will allow the player to direct the shuttle into the opposite court from any position in his own court.

(5) *Preparation, action and recovery.* Often only a limited preparation is possible. As long as the racket head is taken back by wrist action only, then force can be applied to hit the shuttle. Recovery is simply maintaining the state of balance and moving immediately after the stroke.

(6) *Variations in hitting techniques.* All strokes involve the application of force to the shuttle. This force is delivered by the racket head. There are four basic hitting techniques. Any stroke can be analysed in terms of these hitting techniques.

(a) *The 'stroke through' stroke*. The force is applied by the racket hea. The racket face meets the shuttle at right angles to the pathway of the shuttle. The racket head follows through in the direction in which the shuttle was hit. The stroke is very smooth. Examples are the underarm and overhead clears, the flat smash, and the slow drop shot.

(b) *The 'glancing blow 'stroke*. The force is diverted to give the shuttle a glancing blow. Examples are sliced shots, i.e., drops, smashes and net jabs. The stroke is deceptive for a player may prepare to deliver a strong blow to the shuttlecock and then just prior to impact, turn the racket face to deliver a glancing blow. Consequently the shuttle travels slowly through the air or because of the spin, travels a shorter distance if struck with full fo ce.

(c) *The 'impact' stroke*. The force is applied to the shuttle and the racket head stops sharply at the point of impact. There is no follow through. Examples are dab shots and the overhead backhand clear and backhand smash.

(d) *The 'sponge' stroke*. The force is absorbed and the speed is taken off the oncoming shuttle. The racket face gives slightly on impact to slow the shuttle down. It is a stroke played when receiving a very strong smash and control is required to direct the return.

All the basic strokes in the game involve one or a combination of these variations in hitting techniques. Many players have deceptive shots. A player prepares for one sort of stroke and then immediately prior the impact changes the hitting technique to apply the force in a different way. It is a simple matter to prepare for one type of stroke and then to deliver another.

Practice each variation in turn from different positions on the court. From the net or rear court and with underarm and overhead strokes. Try to combine the different strokes. For example combine a 'stroke through/ glancing blow' stroke, or a 'glancing blow/impact' stroke. Deceive your opponent in this way. With practise several new strokes can be developed and added to the range of strokes one has.

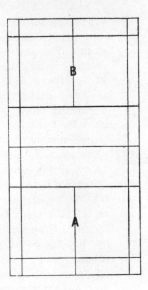

FIG. 23
*First Method* – Rallying Practice.

(1) **A** and **B** stand facing each other in the positions as shown.
(2) **A** serves to **B** and the rally begins.
(3) Both players hit the shuttle at each other.
(4) To hit the shuttle a player is allowed to move one foot only, when necessary.
(5) Try to force the opponent to make a mistake.

Both players will have to be continually adjusting the position of the body to allow freedom of movement of the racket to hit the shuttle.

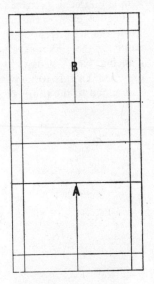

FIG. 24
*Second Method*

The players **A** and **B** stand in the positions as shown.
**A** must remain in his position throughout the practice.
**B** is allowed to move from his position.
**A** hits the shuttle anywhere in the opposite court.
**B** must always return the shuttle to **A**.

The practice begins with **A** serving high to **B**. Each time the rally stops, **A** begins again with a high serve. The practice continues for five minutes and then the players change over.

From any position on court **B** must hit the shuttle back to a pre-determined area, to **A**. This practice forces **B** to learn control of the racket face and become aware of his position in relation to the opposite court. **B** also learns to manipulate his body and to improvise strokes to hit the shuttle to **A**.

With continual practice each player will experience the problem of hitting the shuttle from difficult positions and should show an improvement in performance in the actual game situation.


## 16. ORDER OF LEARNING THE STROKES

The strokes have been discussed in detail. Each stroke can be learned by following the instructions. There are so many basic strokes that it is necessary to have some idea about which ones to learn first. The following order for learning strokes may not suit everyone. The order is arranged according to the normal development of a learner.

A learner gains most satisfaction from playing a rally. He enjoys the pleasure of hitting the shuttle back over the net. This shuttle is usually hit from a high position or a low position with an overhead or underarm stroke.

*Learn and Practise*

(1) The position of readiness.
(2) The forehand grip.
(3) The backhand grip.
(4) The overhead forehand clear.

The shuttle is hit from a high position more often than a low position. From the high position it is hit back high. This stroke is the basis of all overhead strokes.

(5) The underarm forehand low return.
(6) The underarm backhand low return.
(7) The underarm forehand clear.
(8) The underarm backhand clear.

These four strokes can be practised quite easily in the same practice session. The action is identical for both forehand strokes and both backhand strokes. The difference is that the speed of the racket head increases for the clear, prior to impact with the shuttle, and the racket head follows through high to recover.

At this stage it is necessary to play a game. The serve is the first stroke in a game and must be learned.

(9) The short serve.
(10) The high serve.
(11) The overhead forehand smash.

In a game, an attacking stroke is required. Most learners enjoy trying to hit the shuttle down with great force. So learn the basic attacking stroke, the smash.

(12) The overhead forehand drop shot.
This is a variation on the clear and the smash. The same action but a more gentle stroke. Learn both the slow drop shot and the fast drop shot.

(13) The net shots.
In a Badminton club most of the games are Doubles. In Doubles there is a fair amount of net play. Learn the net shots.

(14) Receiving the serve.
The ability to hit the shuttle near the net is a development towards attacking the serve. Begin now to attack the serve.

(15) Flick serves and drive serves.
Learn these variations on the serve.

(16) Forehand drive.

(17) Backhand drive.
Often the shuttle is between the high and low positions. Rather than wait for the shuttle to drop lower, learn to meet the shuttle and drive the shuttle over the net.

The backhand strokes from an overhead position have been left to the end. This is because a learner usually finds it easier to play shots high on the backhand side with a forehand stroke. Now learn the overhead backhand strokes.

(18) The overhead backhand clear.

(19) The overhead backhand drop shot.

(20) The overhead backhand smash.


17. CONCLUSION TO PART ONE
The aim of this section has been to provide clear, concise instructions and advice about the game. The ability to use the correct stroke at the correct time can only be achieved by practice and playing experience. The possible variations in play are too many to be understood when learning the game. If the basic skills are mastered and the principles of tactics understood, there is no doubt that a tremendous amount of enjoyment and satisfaction will be gained from the game of Badminton.

PART TWO

# Training for Badminton

# 18. INTRODUCTION TO PART TWO

Badminton is a game that is increasing in popularity. As facilities improve and people have more leisure time, it has the advantage of being a recreational activity which provides enjoyment and early satisfaction even for the beginner. Both children and adults discover it as an easy game to play, for the simple reason that it is easy to play a rally and gain enjoyment. In schools it is being taught to younger children as a part of the Physical Education curriculum instead of being restricted to a select few as an extra curricular school club activity.

As a major sport in its own right, it is played by many countries who compete at an international level for the Thomas Cup. It has been accepted as a sport in the Commonwealth and Empire Games, and perhaps may develop as an Olympic Sport.

Even with this large increase in the number of players, and the opportunity to play in competitive Badminton at all levels, Badminton remains very much an Amateur sport with an amateurish attitude towards the play. It is this attitude which is at fault. Many sports bodies, i.e. athletics, swimming, rowing, to name but a few, though amateur sports by virtue of their constitutions, adopt almost a professional attitude in their approach to sport. The participants use modern training methods to improve technique and increase strength and fitness. The coaches and competitors in these sports are well aware of the advantages to be gained from applying modern methods in training for the sport. The application of modern training methods in a particular sport have improved standards of performance out of all recognition during the last decade. The actual amount of time spent on practice and training by participants in other sports is no longer than that spent by the badminton enthusiast.

The difference is that other sports are willing to use modern training methods to improve technique, fitness and strength, whereas the badminton player still relies to a large extent on ability only and the playing of games for self improvement. Very few badminton players use modern methods of training and very many do not know anything about modern training methods.

This section attempts to introduce modern training methods to Badminton. It explains what modern training methods are, why they should be used, and how they can be used. It gives a series of specialised training practices which are designed to improve the fitness and performance of any badminton player. It is an attempt to inform players how to train.

## 19. PROGRAMME OF TRAINING FOR BADMINTON PLAYERS

The following programme is designed to improve the overall fitness and level of performance of all badminton players. The programme is in two sections. The first section applies to training *for* the game: the second section applies to training *in* the game. There is a vast difference between these two sections. In all sports, and Badminton is no exception to the rule, it is essential to build up a basic level of fitness before playing the game. This would take the form of pre-season training and requires a full programme of work designed to build a firm foundation of fitness. Once fitness has been attained, the emphasis will be on specialised skill training. Specialised skill training will help the player to maintain and even improve his basic level of fitness, but even more so it will help to improve the skills necessary for the game. The second section, training in the game, is specially designed to achieve the improvement of skill. It takes the form of training sequences. The player will be required to perform continuously a pattern of movement which would occur in the game's situation. By constant repetition of that movement, the skill is perfected and the player improves his stroke, his fitness and his strength. For each stroke in the game of Badminton, there are progressive training sequences. Each stroke under consideration begins with a simple sequence for the school or club player and gradually progresses to more complex sequences for the County and International player. Each sequence used correctly allows the player to develop that part of his game in which lies his weakness. Thus the emphasis may be on control and accuracy, or endurance and speed, or balance or footwork. All these factors can be found in a sequence and the sequence used to develop the particular weakness.

Each sequence is artificial only in that it is isolated from the game and the particular movement pattern or stroke is constantly repeated. However, each sequence is based on a pattern of movement which can and does often happen in a game of Badminton. A player who works at a sequence and develops a particular stroke should have no difficulty in performing that pattern of movement or stroke when confronted with it in the game situation. In fact, by working through all the sequences a player will discover that by performing the correct movement pattern in a game situation, he will be able to increase the number of possible replies to that situation – i.e. a player playing a forehand overhead shot from the forehand corner will be aware of numerous possibilities for his return shot. This is because by the constant repetition under pressure he has been made to experience the identical situation in training and learnt to return many different types of shot from that position. This will be obvious once the training begins.

For the player who wishes to improve at Badminton, whatever the level of attainment, this training programme is essential.

# 20. THE REQUIREMENTS OF A PLAYER

ENDURANCE

All Badminton players must have experienced the point at which they become tired and their game suffers as a result. It is necessary to develop greater endurance or stamina. With greater endurance a player can play for a longer period of time before fatigue sets in. He can perform a greater output of work. The benefits of this are obvious to anyone who has lost a game because he suddenly tired, and endurance training is an essential part of a player's programme. The muscles need strengthening to allow the player to continue his full rate of work for a longer period before fatigue sets in.

This can be achieved by road running and cross-country or by the means of the specially devised training sequences.

The muscles can be strengthened by resistance exercises, based on the principle of overload. By continuous repetition of a set exercise the muscles are worked and muscle endurance is developed.

If the arm is bent and stretched continuously, a point is arrived at when fatigue sets in and the exercise becomes difficult to perform. If a weight of 5 lb. is held in the hand, the load is increased and greater strength is required to bend and stretch the arm until fatigue point is reached. Both exercises build muscle endurance, but greater muscle strength is developed by adding the weight. When training to build up muscle endurance, the more repetitions that can be performed before fatigue, the greater is the endurance.

Endurance can be developed by set exercises and also by special Badminton training exercises.

STRENGTH

Muscle strength is necessary for increasing power and speed. Strength is developed by weight training, in which weights are used to develop certain muscles, or by making use of the body weight.

(a) An exercise is repeated a set number of times. As the exercise becomes easy the weight is increased and strength is built up.

(b) Using the body weight to develop strength is achieved by repeating a specialised badminton exercise until fatigue point and then carrying on beyond fatigue point. The training sequences are designed to develop strength in this way.

MOBILITY

Badminton is a game which makes very severe demands on the body. A player must be able to twist and turn, stretch and bend, etc. The limbs and joints must be able to perform their full range of movement.

*Legs:* A player requires full flexion and extension in his ankles, knees and hips.

71

*Trunk and Shoulders:* Many twisting and stretching movements are required. Full mobility is necessary in the spine, hip and shoulder joints. Exercises are important for increasing the range of movement in these areas. Mobility can be increased by:

(a) Specialised movement technique exercises.

(b) Practices on court which require and develop mobility.

AGILITY

The game demands quickness of movement and good footwork. This is developed by playing games, and performing set sequences which emphasise quick movements.

It is also developed by skipping with particular step patterns.

SPEED OF MOVEMENT

Speed of movement is dependant on two factors:

(a) *Reflexes.* This is the name given to reacting quickly. In fact it relates to degree of skill the player has achieved. It is skill in the game as a whole and not only skilled stroke play. The highly skilled player sees the situation, i.e. position of opponent on court, preparation for the stroke, action of opponent and possible return shot of his opponent. His brain analyses all these factors and selects only those factors which are necessary for that particular situation. The brain sends a message to the muscles which then make the appropriate movement. Reflexes are dependent on the experience of the player in selecting or discarding the impulses received by the brain in many similar situations.

(b) *Strength.* Speed of movement is dependent on strength. If the brain sends a message to the muscles, the muscle must be able to perform the movement required. The greater the strength of the muscles making the movement in proportion to the body weight, the quicker are the movements.

EFFORT QUALITIES

Any movement requires an effort. Though broadly speaking, people use to some degree the correct effort when performing any task, the ability to perform the correct effort at all times is very difficult. For instance, a person would not pick up a cup with the sort of effort required to pick up a bucket of water. The difference is so obvious. Yet in Badminton many players use far more effort than is necessary for a particular stroke. The strong effort in any stroke comes in the actual hitting phase. The preparation and follow through in the stroke require less strength yet how many players actually do this. Many use the same amount of strength and effort throughout the whole stroke. The muscles have no opportunity to relax and the player becomes tired very quickly.

72

At all times during the game a player should be in a state of readiness. The whole body should be carried and not allowed to give into the body weight and slump at all. If possible maintain a feeling of lightness throughout the body. Movement should be light, quick and controlled in moving about the court and in preparing for strokes. An increase in strength and firmness is felt during the moment of action in hitting the shuttle. This applies in a powerful stroke and a delicate touch stroke. Even a delicate touch stroke requires great effort to maintain the fine touch quality. The ability to change in an instance from a strong hitting action to a delicate touch shot without altering the action of the stroke requires great control and appreciation of the correct effort qualities. The ability to do this can be achieved in set practice. The main point at this stage is to always maintain the fine tension throughout the body during the game.

Briefly these are the needs of a badminton player. The training programme is specially designed to cater for these needs.

No mention has been made of the qualities necessary for a champion. It is not the intention of this programme to develop the 'will to win', the 'killer' instinct, the ability to play the right shot at the right time, etc. The mental attitude to the game is a purely personal matter. Whatever the attitude to the game, the following programme is designed to develop the basic needs of a player and to improve performance. If it succeeds in these aims then it has achieved its purpose.

The training programme is in two sections:
(1) Training for the Game.
(2) Training in the Game.

## 21. TRAINING FOR THE GAME

It is essential to build up a basic level of fitness prior to the beginning of the season. Even though many players begin to play the game prior to the start of the season, a heavier training schedule is more effective for establishing this basic level of fitness.

The following programme is for a period of one month and should be performed in addition to pre-season games practice.

ENDURANCE

Endurance training is necessary for increasing the work capacity of the muscles. For players this will take the form of road running or cross country. A satisfactory distance to start with is between three and five miles. Set yourself a course which will cover this distance. Run round the course in the following manner:

Mile 1 – Jog trot and brisk walking.

Mile 2 – Steady pace.
Mile 3 – Jog trot and brisk walking.
During the first week of training take your time and don't work too hard. Many people dislike training because they feel they must push themselves and suffer. It can be enjoyable if there is a gradual build up to fitness. So, enjoy your training. Begin slowly, walk when you are out of breath. Allow your own fitness to dictate your effort. The first task is to cover the distance. It is not essential to feel that you must run yourself into the ground. This involves a mental approach to fitness which can only be achieved when the mind and body have become conditioned to the work.

STRENGTH

Strength is achieved by weight training. Weight training means using weights to develop the strength of certain muscle groups. It is not the intention here to devise a weight training schedule, for it is a very specialised method of building up strength. Each individual requires expert advice and to be shown the correct method of using weights. Incorrect use of weights can be quite harmful. However, these days there are numerous physical educators who are able to plan a personal programme of weight training for any player who wishes to use weights for his strength development. It is enough to say that a player requires strength in his shoulders, abdomen, back and leg muscles. Weight training is an ideal way to build up strength in these muscle groups and the keen enthusiast, the competitor, would benefit a great deal by considering the use of weights in his training programme.

For those players who do not wish to use weights it is essential that certain exercises are performed daily in addition to running. The exercises which follow are useful in developing strength and flexibility. These are exercises which can be performed in the home, and are written out in the form of a training programme.

| | Exercise | Repetitions |
|---|---|---|
| (1) | Press ups | 10 |
| (2) | Sit ups | 20 |
| (3) | Squats | 25 |
| (4) | Back bends | 5 |
| (5) | Squat thrust | 10 |
| (6) | Step ups | 15 |

A description of these exercises follows:
*Press ups:* Lie face downwards on the floor. Place the palms of the hands on the floor at the side of the shoulders. Keep the body still and straighten the arms to raise the body off the floor. This is a press-up. Lower the body

74

by bending the arms and repeat the action according to the number of times set in the programme.

*Sit ups:* Lie on the back, legs straight and feet under a support, i.e. chair, bed, etc. Hands clasped behind the head. Keeping the legs straight, raise the upper body so that the elbows touch the knees. Lower the body to the position of lying on the back. This is one sit-up. This movement develops strength in the abdominal muscles.

*Squats:* Stand upright. Keep body erect, head up, and lower the seat and body by bending the knees into a squat position. Stand up again. This action is a squat. It develops the thigh muscles.

*Back bends:* Lie on the front, hands clasped behind the head and elbows raised. Raise the upper body off the ground by working the muscles of the back. Hold position and lower to the ground. This is a back bend.

*Squat thrust:* Stand upright. Lower the body into the squat position. Place the palms of the hands on to the ground to take the body weight. Thrust the legs straight backwards until you are now in a press up position. Bring the legs back to the squat position and stand up. This is a squat thrust. This movement should be done quickly and smoothly without a pause between the change of positions.

*Step ups:* Place a chair or bench in front of you. Step up on to it and stand up straight. Step down again. This is a step up and develops the lower leg muscles.

To perform this programme of six exercises go through from 1 to 6 completing the repetitions required. Do this daily and make a habit of it.

## FOUR WEEK TRAINING PROGRAMME
*Week 1*
3 Mile Run daily from Monday to Saturday.
Exercise programme of 6 exercises one to six once through in order.
Repeat this programme daily from Monday to Saturday.
Leave Sunday for a rest day.
*Week 2*
3 Mile Run.
Exercise programme of six exercises. Perform one to six twice through in the correct order.
Do this daily from Monday to Saturday.
*Week 3*
4 Mile Run.
Exercise programme of six exercises. Perform from one to six twice through in the correct order.
Do them daily from Monday to Saturday.
*Week 4*
5 Mile Run.

75

Exercise programme of six exercises. Perform from one to six three times through in correct order.
Do this daily from Monday to Saturday.

COMMENTS ON PROGRAMME
The programme is a basic one, gradually building up into more demanding work from the person training. A six day programme is the aim. If it is not possible to complete a six day programme, a minimum programme should be at least four days a week. If it is not possible to build up the amount of work required over the four week period, stick to the first week's schedule for all the four weeks. The keen player will try to complete the programme. Those players who are unable to complete the whole programme should still train as much as possible. A little exercise done regularly is better than an enormous amount done once in a while with large gaps in the training routine. The programme is within the scope of any healthy person, and for this reason it is very basic. It is not possible in this book to devise a personal training programme for every player. Use this one as a basis and if you wish to do more ask the advice of a specialist physical educator or athletics coach.

## GENERAL EXERCISES AND TRAINING
The content of this section deals with general exercises which can be used as an addition to the set training programme. If you wish to develop flexibility and muscle strength then select a few of these to add to your basic programme.

SKIPPING
Skipping is a form of exercise used by many games players to develop footwork. Skipping can become boring, and a way of overcoming monotony is to skip to music. Any music with a regular rhythm to it is good for skipping. 'Pop' music is excellent. It is easier to get into a rhythm and appears less tiring. There are several ways of using skipping as an exercise. One method is to skip to 100 turns of the rope and then rest a minute. Repeat this until 1,000 turns of the rope have been completed.

A second method is to skip for a certain amount of time and rest for a certain amount of time. Select a period of 12 minutes skipping.

Skip for 2 minutes. Rest 1 minute.

Repeat this six times until 12 minutes' skipping has been completed. If one minute is not long enough for a rest, have a two minute rest. The rest period depends on the individual.

The third method is to skip non-stop for the period of time selected, i.e. 10 minutes of skipping. Skip for the 10 minutes non-stop. This requires tremendous fitness and is not a method to select unless one is really fit.

# GENERAL EXERCISES
## ABDOMINAL AND THIGH MUSCLES
### (1)

1 Back lying    2 Knees to chest    3 Straighten legs    4 Lower
               quickly

Repeat this exercise 10 times.

### (2)

1 Back lying   2 Raise body and legs to   3 Lower
            touch toes with fingers

Repeat this exercise 10 times.

### (3) KANGAROO JUMP

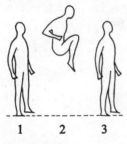

1      2      3

Repeat 10 times without stopping.

### (4) COSSACK JUMP

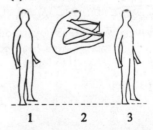

1      2      3

Repeat 10 times without stopping.

(5) SQUAT JUMP

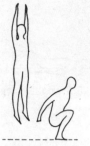
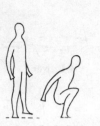

1 Stand  2 Squat    3 Jump  4 Squat
                    and
                    Stretch

Repeat 10 times without stopping.


(6) FLEXIBILITY

1 Back lying with legs straight. 2 Raise both legs together and lift over head to touch floor. 3 Lower slowly into starting position.

Repeat 10 times.


(7) TRUNK BENDING

1 Back lying    2 Move upper body    3 Return to
                and squeeze head down  starting position
                     to knees          slowly

Repeat 10 times.

(8)

1 Begin with legs apart (straight legs). 2 Squeeze elbows down between knees until they touch the floor (keeping legs straight). 3 Return to original position.

Repeat 10 times.

(9) SPINE FLEXIBILITY

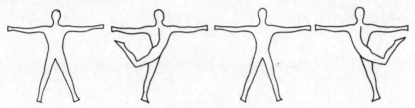

Front lying – arms and legs apart. Bring right foot across to touch left hand. Keep the shoulders on the ground. Repeat on left side. Perform 10 times.

(10) BACK STRENGTHENER (Seesaw)

Rocking from chest to thighs. 10 times.

(11) LUNGE JUMPS

Bounce in this position 1, 2, 3, 4, and on 5th bounce change to opposite leg.

79

## (12) TRUNK CIRCLING

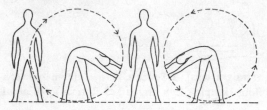

Circle body round from waist. In front of body to side and behind the body. 5 times to left, 5 times to right.


## (13) SHOULDER GIRDLE

1 Arms circling backwards. Inside of arms touching ears as they circle past the head. A full circle.

2 Bend and place arms on chair. Squeeze shoulders back, keeping spine straight. Squeeze and release 10 times.


All these exercises can be performed daily to increase strength and flexibility, and range of movement. It is not necessary to perform all the exercises from the beginning. Select several and do each two or three times, but do them with daily regularity. It will not be possible to achieve the full range of movement from the beginning. However if performed with daily regularity, after several weeks, the range of movement will be increased and the numbers of times it is possible to perform each exercise will be increased.

## 22. TRAINING IN THE GAME

It is true to say that the majority of players practise their Badminton. The usual type of practice is a 'knock-up' i.e. a few overhead clears, backhand clears, drop shots and smashes, etc. The idea is to get warmed up and then play games, Singles or Doubles. The ambitious players enter tournaments, play in matches, and improve in this manner by gaining greater experience. This approach is quite sound, but not positive enough. A more positive or scientific approach is required and progressive training methods must be developed if a training session is to be meaningful. Very few badminton players really know how to train and practise. For positive results, training must take the form of logical progressive practices. The 'knock-up' and game attitude lacks real purpose. There is no guarantee that a weakness in the player's game will be worked on and improved. The opportunity to improve the weakness in a game may occur a few times only. There is a great need for more positive training methods, and more intense practices.

This section is designed to give a more positive and scientific approach to practice. It is the most important section as practice and training are best performed in conditions similar to playing conditions. The following practices are designed to improve:

> Endurance
> Strength
> Mobility
> Speed
> Balance and Footwork
> Stroke production
> Control and accuracy.

Simply the aim is to improve the fitness and the skill of the player. During a game there are certain patterns of play which keep re-curring. Whatever the situation of a player on the court there are several definite possible returns of shot in each situation. The aim is to perform these specialised skill training exercises which compel the player to make all the possible returns. Each stroke and each situation has been isolated from the game situation. During a game there is always a pattern of movement required to travel into position from the central base, play a shot, and return to the central base. In the game, hundreds of these movement patterns flow into one another to make up the game. The idea is to isolate each individual movement pattern and compel the player to repeat it many times. By doing so, the player will develop in his body the appropriate movements to play in a situation should it occur during a game.

Many players have practised isolated strokes, the smash, forehand and backhand clear, the drop shot, etc. By performing the action many times, they learn to 'groove the stroke', until it becomes an automatic action. The

81

same idea is developed here to a greater extent. Instead of one isolated stroke being practised, the emphasis is on a complete pattern of movement being practised. In this section, the pattern of movement is called a sequence. A sequence consists of the starting position, travelling to the hitting position, preparation, hitting action, follow through and recovery. Each stroke and pattern of movement is practised by working on simple sequences and progressing to more complex sequences as the level of performance improves. Repetition of a sequence not only trains the appropriate pattern of movement necessary in a situation but develops to a higher degree the requirements of a player. By correct use of the sequence, balance and footwork, stroke production, control and accuracy will be improved. By increasing the number of times each sequence is performed, the work load and work rate is increased, and the player will improve his endurance, strength, mobility and speed.

THE TRAINING SEQUENCE

There is nothing complicated in each sequence. Each one is self-explanatory and easy to understand. It is not necessary to work through all the sequences on any particular stroke. Some players need to begin with a simple sequence, others may begin with a more complex sequence. The choice is dependent on the ability and fitness of the individual player.

As stated previously, the aim of each sequence is to improve the requirements of a player, endurance, strength, speed, mobility, footwork and balance, control and accuracy. A balanced combination of all these factors developed to the full potential of the player is the end result of this training.

It is not to be expected that each factor will develop at the same rate as the others. If endurance and strength are low, the balance will be upset and control and accuracy will suffer as the player becomes fatigued. If stroke production and control and accuracy are not of a sufficient standard, then the player, being unable to use the full distance of the court with his strokes, will not have to travel as far and will be unable to develop his strength and endurance to the maximum.

These difficulties can be overcome by correct use of the sequence. The following discusses the correct use of the sequence.

THE FEEDER

The feeder has a very responsible task. He dictates the sequence. He must read the instructions for each sequence very carefully and understand his task. If the player is to gain the full benefit of the training, the feeder must concentrate on good control and accurate placing of the shuttlecock.

The feeder is able to dictate the pace of a sequence. He can slow it down by hitting the shuttle on a high pathway or speed it up by increasing the pace of the shuttle, and hitting it on a lower pathway. The position of the feeder is the target for the player. In between shots the feeder must remain in his fixed position as shown in the diagram of each sequence. Even though he has to move away from his fixed position to return a poor shot from the player, he should return quickly to his fixed position. This is important, as any unnecessary movements in between shots tend to distract the player and result in the breakdown of the sequence. The feeder must be aware of this and should concentrate, and aim at control and accurate placements.

THE PLAYER

In all the sequences the player under pressure is named **A**. For the purpose of this explanation he will be known as the player **A**. The player **A** selects the stroke he wishes to practise and the sequence at which he wishes to begin training. If the player **A** finds a particular sequence is too difficult in technique or too demanding physically then return to a simpler sequence. The player **A** must work at his own level of performance. It may be necessary to experiment at first to discover what that level is. Read through the uses of a sequence and decide what factors of the game require improving for yourself. If it is endurance and strength be certain to inform the feeder **B** of your requirements and the feeder **B** can feed the appropriate shots to you.

Do not 'cut corners'; always complete the full range of movement and the correct movement pattern. Aim at accurate placements and returns. Set yourself a schedule which can be completed adequately each session. To help in this read the section on training schedules.

Concentrate on the task in hand, be prepared for hard work, and fitness and skill will show a definite improvement.

THE COUNTER

In all sequences where a counter is shown, the counter will be known as **C**.

The task of the counter **C** is to keep a score of the sequence. This becomes especially difficult in the complex training sequence involving three or four strokes. The feeder and player must concentrate on maintaining the sequence and the counter must keep the score. The counter can also assist by informing the players **A** and **B**, if strokes are not being performed correctly or if returns are not accurate enough.

The task is two-fold. Keep the score and insist on correct use of the sequence.

It should be noted that the order of play in a sequence is such that the player **A** has a rest by becoming the counter. In any sequence the three players rotate. Feeding is good for warming up, which leads to the hard work as player, which leads to the rest period as counter.

It is not necessary to have a counter, but it does allow play to be continuous with just sufficient rest to allow the player **A** to maintain work for longer periods. Work, rest, work, rest, etc. will allow a higher standard of performance to be achieved during the work period, than if the player **A** works without ceasing before fatigue prevents him continuing.

## WORK LOAD

Work load is the quantity of work the player sets out to achieve. The section on training schedules will explain this in more detail. Simply the player may set himself the task of completing a repetition of 10 sequences. This is his work load. As he gets stronger and fitter he may increase his work load to a repetition of 20 sequences. The limit is set only by the player's ability to withstand the onset of fatigue.

## WORK RATE

Work rate is the time allowed to perform a given quantity of work. A player may wish to perform a repetition of 10 sequences and allows himself 2 minutes. He must work at a certain rate to achieve this amount of work in the time allowed. As he gets fitter and stronger, he may decide to reduce the time to 10 sequences in one minute. To achieve this task he must speed up and increase his rate of work. He has to achieve a given amount of work in less time. Greater effort is needed and he reaches fatigue much sooner.

The combination of work load and work rate and their application, is an essential factor in increasing fitness.

In the game of Badminton, work rate can be increased by hitting the shuttle on a lower arc through the air and thereby reducing the amount of time the shuttle takes to travel from one position to the other. The sequence is speeded up. Work rate can be decreased by hitting the shuttle higher and allowing more time for it to travel from one position to the other. The sequence is slowed down.

It is essential that both the feeder and the player realise this fact and make use of this when playing a sequence. It is important, for it has a direct relationship on developing the basic requirements of the player.

## ENDURANCE

Endurance is the ability to withstand the onset of fatigue. If a player desires to increase his endurance then he must increase his work load. Perhaps fatigue is reached after ten repetitions of a training sequence, which is performed at a certain speed. If the sequence is slowed down by hitting the shuttle higher, the player may be able to perform fifteen repetitions of that sequence before the fatigue point is reached. The work load is increased and endurance is developed. By constant training and emphasis on increasing the number of repetitions in a sequence, the player will gradually improve his endurance and be able to work for a longer period of time before the fatigue point is reached.

## STRENGTH

A certain amount of muscle strength is built up in the same manner as endurance is improved. Strength can be achieved by increasing the amount of work to be performed. If at the same time the rate of work is increased so that the muscles have less time to perform the same amount of work, greater strength is acquired over a period of training. To develop strength increase the number of repetitions of a sequence or increase the speed at which the repetitions must be performed.

## SPEED

Speed of movement can be developed by increasing the work rate.

It is inevitable that by practising the sequences there will be an improvement in endurance, strength and speed. By altering the emphasis slightly in each sequence, one or other of these three factors may be developed at a higher rate than the others.

## MOBILITY

Mobility is the ability to reach the full range of movement in the joints. It is not necessary to try to develop mobility in the training sequences. To perform each sequence correctly demands and compels the player to increase the range of movement in his limbs. There is so much stretching and twisting, etc. that the player cannot help but increase mobility.

## BALANCE AND FOOTWORK

This training programme does not intend to teach balance and footwork. However the aim is to perform each sequence correctly. Correct performance means getting the body weight behind the shuttle and to do this good balance is essential. There are numerous movement patterns to be practised. To perform them a player will experience a whole range of complex step patterns. By practice, balance and footwork will improve. The method of travelling from one position to another will depend on the player. The sequences compel the player to select correct movements to travel about the court.

## CONTROL AND ACCURACY

Repetition of a sequence allows the player the opportunity to play a shot to a fixed target. To reach the target will require control and accuracy. The fact that there is a target (the feeder) to aim at allows the player to judge how accurate he is. Control is linked with accuracy because though a player may hit a shuttle in the right direction, he must also hit it with just enough strength to send it to the target. Continual repetition of the same stroke as performed in the sequence, gives the player time to judge how much strength is required to hit the shuttle a certain distance.

Control and accuracy is improved by regular practice in training sequences.

The first aim is to give the training a purpose. Select the stroke which requires improving. There are specialised training sequences for every stroke so this is not difficult. If you are an average club or school player it is wise to begin with a simple sequence and progress at your own rate. For the County and International player it may be wise to select a more complex sequence. The choice is a personal one. However there is no reason why even an International player may not select a simple sequence for the perfection of stroke production. As an example, the stroke selected may be the forehand overhead clear. The player decides to begin at the Tenth sequence which is a forehand overhead clear from the forehand and backhand corners to the opposite forehand corner. Player **A** must make two shots to complete a sequence.

If the emphasis is on stroke production, control and accuracy, both the player **A** and the feeder **B** should hit high defensive clears to allow more time for the correct stroke to be played. If the emphasis is on strength and speed, increase the work rate by hitting an attacking clear which travels on a lower arc and allows less time to play the stroke. If player **A** is slow travelling back for a stroke, feeder **B** plays an attacking clear which forces **A** to speed up when travelling backwards. Player **A** returns with a high clear.

If player **A** is slow returning to his base he should hit an attacking clear which forces him to return to his centre quickly. Feeder **B** feeds a high clear to allow **A** time to travel to the hitting position and gain a slight rest before rushing into the centre again. The whole pace of the sequence can be altered to compel the player to work on a weakness.

The player selects the number of repetitions he is able to perform to a satisfactory standard before the onset of fatigue. It may be that fatigue begins after ten repetitions of a sequence. If this is the case, practise the sequence until ten repetitions are performed without fatigue. Once this number becomes easy to perform, increase the number of repetitions up to fifteen. With continual work in this manner the strength and fitness will increase and also the ability to perform more repetitions.

When the session is limited to work on one particular sequence, the order of play (feeder, player, counter), can be rotated three or four times instead of once only. The player will improve fitness and control on that particular stroke to a greater degree.

The idea should be work through several sequences in a training session. An hour spent in this way prior to normal games will give the player a fair quantity of work to accomplish. It will improve his fitness to a greater extent than normal training and improve his technical skill.

The main aim of this programme is to enable any player to play a game at a faster pace for a longer period of time. A player who can perform all the sequences should be able to perform the correct body movements for

86

any situation which may occur during a game.

However it would be foolish to expect to develop into a highly skilled player by practising these sequences only. They are to help you to perform the stroke you decide is necessary, in a successful manner and return it accurately to the area you select. They are a means to an end. Complete skill in the game can only come from playing the game. The sequences improve technique and ability to perform strokes under pressure. They cannot teach you to win, but it is certainly good for the confidence, when you realise that you can perform an appropriate stroke in any situation and keep doing this for a long period of time.

Though all the sequences are taken from situations which are to be experienced in a game, they are artificial because of their isolation and repetition of the same pattern of movement.

After a training session on the sequences it is sound policy to play a normal game of singles and doubles. In this way the movement patterns will not be allowed to become stereotyped.

These specialised training exercises which develop fitness and technique are used only to improve your game. Remember this when training.

## 23. TRAINING SEQUENCES
## (a) OVERHEAD FOREHAND CLEAR

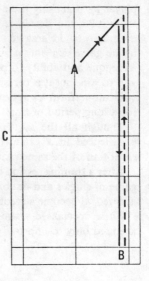

FIG. 25
Forehand clear from backhand corner to opposite
forehand corner. Direction down the line.
Feeder **B** begins sequence with a high serve to **A** from
nearer net. After serve **B** moves back to position as
shown on diagram.
**B** is the feeder and hits high clears to backhand of **A**.
**A** is under pressure, moves to backhand corner,
plays a forehand overhead clear directly to **B** and
then returns to centre.
This is one sequence. Each sequence to be repeated
continuously until the number set by the player is
reached.
Each time **A** must return to the central position.
**C** is the counter and counts the number of sequences.
At finish of exercise the players rotate.
**A** takes the place of **C**.
**B** takes the place of **A**.
**C** takes the place of **B**.
Repeat until all the players have performed sequences
in turn.

*Work Schedule:* Begin with a minimum of 10
repetitions of the sequence. Aim at reaching a
number of 50 repetitions.


*Comments:* **A** must get behind the shuttle and in a position sideways on to
the shuttle. The footwork pattern is personal to the player, and good if the
player is able to position himself correctly for the hitting action.

88

FIG. 26
Overhead forehand clear from centre to opposite
forehand corner. Repeat as in previous sequence.

*Work Schedule*
Minimum of 10 repetitions.
Maximum of 50 repetitions.

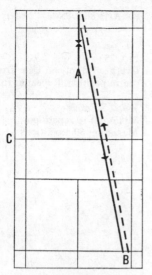

THIRD SEQUENCE

FIG. 27
Forehand clear from forehand corner to opposite
forehand corner. Difficult as **A** hits on the long
diagonal across the court. Repeat as for previous
sequence.

*Work Schedule*
Player should set himself work from 10 repetitions
to 50 repetitions.

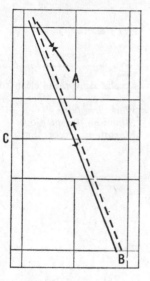

*Comment:* **A** must move quickly to get behind the shuttle in a sideways
position, with weight on the rear foot. This is essential as repetition of the
correct movement pattern will enable **A** to play a greater variety of returns
from the correct position in the normal game situation. There will be a
tendency to position oneself face on to the shuttle under pressure, but if
possible this should be avoided for the reason mentioned.

89

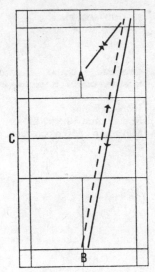

FIG. 28
Overhead forehand clear from backhand corner to centre position. Repeat as for previous sequence.

*Work Schedule*
Minimum 10 repetitions.
Maximum 50 repetitions.

FIFTH SEQUENCE

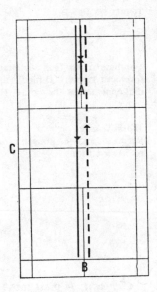

FIG. 29
Forehand overhead clear from centre to centre.

*Work Schedule*
Minimum 10 repetitions.
Maximum 50 repetitions.

*Comment:* This is a very basic sequence. The usual tendency is for **A** to play the stroke in an open body position. **A** must take a sideways position to the shuttle, which will allow him the opportunity for a greater range of strokes in the identical game situation.

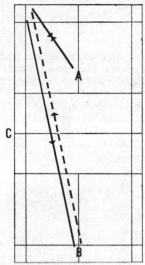

FIG. 30
Forehand overhead clear from forehand corner to
centre.

*Work Schedule*
Minimum 10 repetitions.
Maximum 50 repetitions.

    *Comment:* **A** must try to position himself sideways to the shuttle with
weight on the rear foot before making the shot. This allows him to hit into
the shuttle from a balanced position and move easily back to his central base.

FIG. 31
Forehand overhead clear from backhand corner to opposite backhand corner. The long diagonal. Balance and footwork important.

*Work Schedule*
Minimum 10 repetitions.
Maximum 50 repetitions.

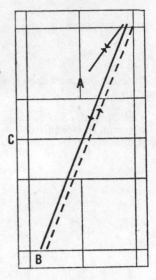

*Comment:* **A** has more time to position himself as the shuttle has a longer distance to travel. **A** must get behind the shuttle weight on the back foot. Stroke demands greater mobility in spine and shoulders and good footwork and balance to hit the shuttle the full distance.

FIG. 32
Forehand overhead clear from central position to opposite backhand corner. Repeat as in previous sequence.

*Work Schedule*
Minimum 10 repetitions.
Maximum 50 repetitions.

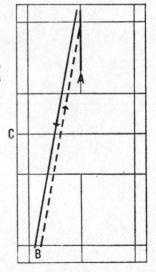

92

FIG. 33
Forehand overhead clear from forehand corner to
opposite backhand corner. Down the line.

*Work Schedule*
Minimum 10 repetitions.
Maximum 50 repetitions.

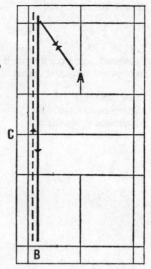

Comment: Correct positioning behind shuttle, weight on rear foot is
important. Control and accuracy should be emphasised as there is very little
margin for error.

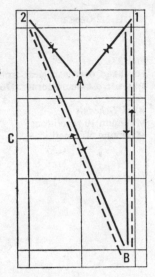

FIG. 34
Forehand clear from forehand and backhand corners to opposite forehand corner.

*Work Schedule*
Minimum 10 repetitions.
Maximum 40 repetitions.

*Comment:* Emphasis on twisting the body, and balance. From backhand corner straight down the line requires good balance and greater flexibility of the spine. From forehand corner covering the diagonal of the court requires good positioning and footwork to get weight behind shot and place enough power behind shuttle (shuttle speed).

ELEVENTH SEQUENCE

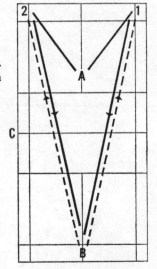

FIG. 35
Forehand overhead clear from forehand and backhand corners to opposite centre. Repeat as in previous sequence.

*Work Schedule*
Minimum 10 repetitions.
Maximum 40 repetitions.

94

FIG. 36
Forehand overhead clear from backhand corner and
forehand corner to opposite backhand corner.

*Work Schedule*
Minimum 10 repetitions.
Maximum 40 repetitions.

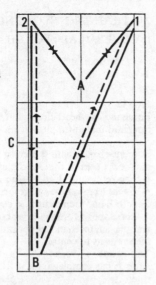

   *Comment:* An overhead forehand clear from backhand corner to opposite
backhand corner along the diagonal requires perfect balance and positioning.
Very demanding on the player in flexibility and strength, especially as fatigue
point is reached.


COMMENTS ON FOREHAND SEQUENCES
All sequences involve intricate footwork patterns but at International and
County level this can be left to the choice of the individual. It is important
that the point of arrival to hit the shuttle is correct. This requires good balance
and correct body positioning and control of the racket face. Direction of
stroke is achieved by positioning the body correctly to enable the shuttle to
be hit easily and directly along line of racket face or by deflecting the wrist
during the hitting phase to place the racket face pointing towards the chosen
pathway of the shuttlecock.
   The emphasis is on control and accuracy, correct positioning and returning
to the central base after the hitting action has been completed. The player
must travel the full distance set in each sequence. The work schedule begins
with 10 repetitions. With regular training the player should be able to increase
the number of repetitions. The limit of repetitions is when fatigue point is
reached. Regular training will enable the player to perform an increased
number of repetitions before fatigue point is reached.

## 24. TRAINING SEQUENCES
### (b) OVERHEAD FOREHAND CLEAR AND UNDERARM CLEAR

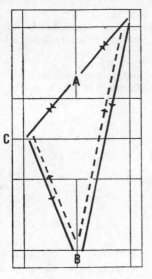

FIG. 37
Forehand overhead clear from backhand corner and
forehand underarm clear from forehand net corner.

Sequence begins with **B** serving a high serve from the
mid-court area to the backhand corner of **A**.
**B** then returns to fixed position as shown.
**A** moves from centre and returns forehand overhead
clear to **B** and then returns to centre position. **B** plays
a drop shot to forehand net corner of **A**. **A** lunges
and plays a forehand underarm clear back to **B** and
then returns to centre.
This is one sequence.
After **A** has completed his work schedule the players
rotate.
**B** takes the place of **A**.
**C** takes the place of **B**.
**A** takes the place of **C** and counts sequences.
This is repeated until each player has had a turn as
player, feeder and counter.
*Work Schedule*
Minimum 10 repetitions.
Maximum 40 repetitions.

*Comments:* It is important that **A** gets behind the shuttle for the overhead
clear. This will allow him to return quickly to his central base. He should
return the drop shot by lunging forwards, weight on the forward leg. After
completing the underarm clear, push off the forward leg to return to the
centre base. This is a strenuous sequence and involves stretching and bending
from **A** in the upper body and an increased amount of leg work. Perform the
work schedule according to the requirements of **A**. Read the introduction
i.e. **B** should clear high to allow **A** time to move into the correct position.

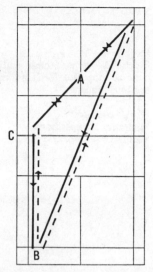

FIG. 38
Forehand overhead clear and forehand underarm clear to opposite backhand corner. Repeat as in previous sequence.

*Work Schedule*
Minimum 10 repetitions.
Maximum 40 repetitions.

*Comment:* **A** must move quickly to reach correct position. He has to return the shuttle along the diagonal of the court, which requires more strength. This becomes difficult as fatigue point is reached. Accuracy is required for the underarm clear down the line as the margin for error is reduced.

Fɪɢ. 39
Forehand overhead clear and forehand underarm
clear to opposite forehand corner. Repeat as in
previous sequence.

*Work Schedule*
Minimum 10 repetitions.
Maximum 40 repetitions.

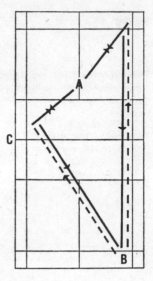

*Comment:* **B** must hit a high defensive clear to backhand corner of **A** to
allow time to return from the forehand net corner.

TEACHING POINTS
In all the three previous sequences, the method of travel to the backhand
corner is dependent on the individual's own choice. However, the arrival
must be at a position sideways to the shuttle with the weight on the rear foot.
In these practices correct positioning is an important factor, even though in
the game's situation it is not always possible to arrive in the correct position.
The reply to the drop shot is either a lunge forward from the central position
or steps which take the player nearer to the shuttle. In a high pressure
sequence the lunge forward may save time in travelling though some players
prefer to move right up to the shuttle, finding it easier to maintain balance
in this way. The lunge forward is a stretch forwards with the weight on the
forward leg (knee flexed to maintain balance), and the rear leg is stretched.
The player returns to the central position by pushing back off the front leg
after playing his shot. This movement is good for developing leg strength.

The different methods of using the sequence to improve different factors
can be obtained by reading the section which deals with 'Uses of a Sequence'
(page 86).

98

FIG. 40
Forehand overhead clear from forehand corner and underarm backhand clear of a drop shot from backhand net corner to opposite centre.

Sequence commences with high service from **B** to forehand corner of **A**.

*Work Schedule*
Minimum 10 repetitions.
Maximum 40 repetitions.

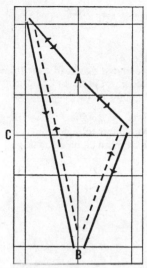

*Comment:* In travelling back to forehand corner **A** must position himself behind the shuttle to gain complete control. This is because the arm movement of the forehand is against the natural movement of the arm and shoulder joint and it becomes extremely difficult to return the shuttle to the centre if it is behind the body. The player must concentrate on getting his body position behind the shuttle so that he may hit forwards, into the shuttle.

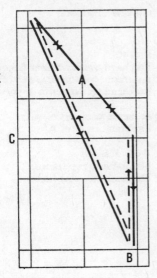

FIG. 41
Forehand overhead clear from forehand corner and underarm backhand clear from backhand net corner to opposite forehand corner.

*Work Schedule*
Minimum 10 repetitions.
Maximum 40 repetitions.

*Comment:* Good positioning necessary for overhead clear to return shuttle along the full diagonal of the court. Accuracy and control required for underarm clear, as shot is down the line and there is less margin for error. The body positioning is essential for the reason described in the previous sequence.

100

FIG. 42
Forehand overhead clear from forehand corner and underarm clear from backhand corner to opposite backhand corner.

*Work Schedule*
Minimum 10 repetitions.
Maximum 40 repetitions.

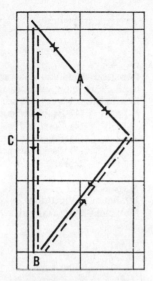

Comment: Accuracy and control required for overhead clear. The shot down the line leaves less margin for error. Player **A** must travel quickly back to rear court for the shot as shuttle travel takes less time from **B** to reach forehand corner of **A**. Shot is down the line.

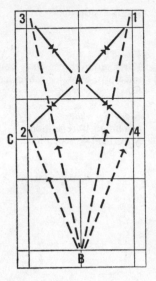

FIG. 43
Forehand clears and underarm forehand and backhand clears to opposite centre.
Combination of previous sequences.
A pathway (1) Backhand corner to centre.
　　　　　(2) Forehand net corner to centre.
　　　　　(3) Forehand deep corner to centre.
　　　　　(4) Backhand net corner to centre and
　　　　　repeat.

*Work Schedule*
Minimum 10 repetitions.
Maximum 30 repetitions.

Comment: After every stroke **A** must return to the centre. **C** should keep
a careful count.

The sequence must be followed in the correct order as the order emphasises
precise movement patterns. The emphasis is on a forward pathway from **1** to
**2** and from **3** to **4**. This is not so difficult. The backward pathways from
**2** to the centre to **3** require a change of direction. This applies also from
**4** to **1**. Emphasis is on good footwork and balance to change direction from
one pathway to another.

102

Fig. 44
Forehand clears and underarm forehand and backhand clears to opposite forehand corner.

*Work Schedule*
Minimum 10 repetitions.
Maximum 30 repetitions.

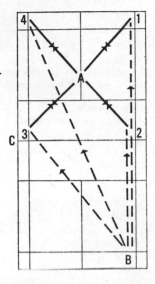

*Comment:* The order of play in the sequence emphasises quick changes of direction from one situation to the next. For this reason, to develop good footwork it is essential that the player returns to his central position after each stroke and does not cut 'corners'.

The changes of direction are quite obvious in the diagram. From position **1** to position **2** the pathway is forwards with a sharp change of direction to the left. From **2** to **3** the pathway is backwards and then a change of direction forwards. From **3** to **4** the pathway is backwards involving a change of direction to the right. From **4** to **1** the pathway is forwards and changing direction to backwards travelling.

As the repetitions are increased and the player becomes fatigued it becomes difficult for the player to perform these changes of direction and still maintain a good standard of footwork and balance. The ability to do this requires a high standard of fitness which is developed by constant repetition of this complex sequence.

103

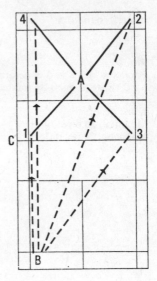

FIG. 45
Forehand clears and underarm forehand and backhand clears to opposite backhand corner.

*Work Schedule*
Minimum 10 repetitions.
Maximum 30 repetitions.

*Comment:* **A** has to travel backwards from net corner to diagonally opposite corner.

There is a change of direction on the forward pathway from **2** to **3** and **4** to **1**. This training exercise is very demanding on the fitness of the player and requires good footwork and balance.

## 25. TRAINING SEQUENCES

### (c) OVERHEAD FOREHAND DROP SHOTS

The first sequences will deal with slow drop shots or floaters. These require more height and a certain amount of deception. Accuracy is essential for the shuttle must drop steeply and close to the net. The aim is not so much to make an outright winner but rather to create an opening and gain the initiative.

* Drop shots are hit (*a*) flat
        (*b*) sliced
        (*c*) reverse sliced

Both sliced shots are really brushing movements of the racket face across the shuttle. The sequences are designed to develop variety on the drop shot.

* *Flat drop Shots.* This is the name given to the stroke in which the racket face meets the shuttle face on. There is an immediate impact.

*Sliced Drop Shots.* The usual type of overhead drop shot. In the normal throwing action the racket face will travel forwards and across the shuttle in

104

a direction from left to right. The strings of the racket stay on the shuttle for a fraction of time longer than in the normal flat drop and give more control.

*Reverse Slice Drop Shot.* The idea is the same as above, but the racket face moves across the shuttle from right to left, in the action. During the sequences, these three drop shots are used. The choice is up to the player, but the possiblity of choice has been mentioned.

OVERHEAD FOREHAND DROP SHOTS. FAST

When performing fast drop shots, the following points apply:

(1) Repeat sequences as for slow drops.

(2) **B** to move his base to point behind service line.

(3) **A** to direct the shuttle downwards. (More use of wrist required).

In both types of drop shot it is essential that **A** positions himself behind the shuttle and in a sideways position. By doing so, the drop shot is disguised to a certain extent. The player receiving would expect a variety of possible returns from a correct position. If **A** allows the shuttle to get behind him, an experienced player will recognise the fact that **A** has a limited number of replies, one of which could be a badly performed drop shot. The player **A** must strive to reach the correct position in all the following drop shot sequences for this reason.

FIRST SEQUENCE

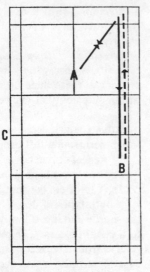

FIG. 46
From backhand corner deep to opposite forehand
net corner, slow drop shot.

**B** feeds high clear to backhand corner of **A**.
**A** moves from centre to backhand corner and plays
a forehand drop shot to opposite forehand net
corner and then returns to centre. **B** returns drop
with high clear and sequence is repeated.

*Work Schedule*
Minimum 10 repetitions.
Maximum 50 repetitions.

*Comment:* The action of the racket face on the shuttle can be flat or a
sliced brush shot. **A** must take up position sideways on to the shuttle.

SECOND SEQUENCE

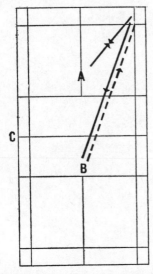

FIG. 47
Backhand corner to centre net.

*Work Schedule*
Minimum 10 repetitions.
Maximum 50 repetitions.

*Comment:* **A** plays stroke with reverse slice (open racket face), or a flat
shot. Requires good balance and footwork and strength to maintain fine
touch necessary for this stroke.

106

FIG. 48
From backhand corner to opposite backhand net corner.

*Work Schedule*
Minimum 10 repetitions.
Maximum 50 repetitions.

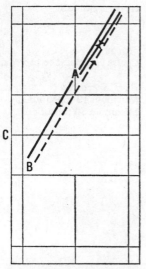

*Comment:* Cross court drop shot. Reverse slice with open racket face – very effective. Can also be hit flat, though not as much control obtained. Balance and correct positioning important. Body is in a more open position, though weight is behind the shuttle.

FOURTH SEQUENCE

FIG. 49
From centre rear court to opposite forehand net corner.

*Work Schedule*
Minimum 10 repetitions.
Maximum 50 repetitions.

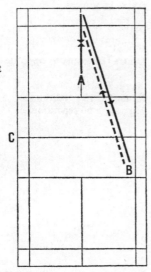

*Comment:* **A** hits flat floating drop or sliced brush shot.

107

FIG. 50
Centre rear court to centre net.

*Work Schedule*
Minimum 10 repetitions.
Maximum 50 repetitions.

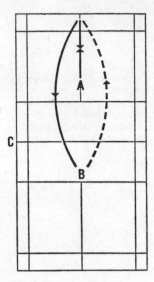

*Comment:* Flat face open drop shot. Usually used as an alternative to the smash, in which lies the deception. Otherwise it is too obvious a stroke and easy to return.

SIXTH SEQUENCE

FIG. 51
Centre rear court to opposite backhand corner.

*Work Schedule*
Minimum 10 repetitions.
Maximum 50 repetitions.

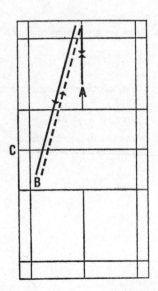

*Comment:* **A** performs flat or reversed slice drop shot.

FIG. 52
Forehand deep corner to opposite forehand net corner.

*Work Schedule*
Minimum 10 repetitions.
Maximum 50 repetitions.

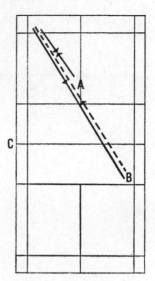

*Comment:* **A** plays sliced drop shot.

EIGHTH SEQUENCE

FIG. 53
Forehand deep corner to opposite centre net.

*Work Schedule*
Minimum 10 repetitions.
Maximum 50 repetitions.

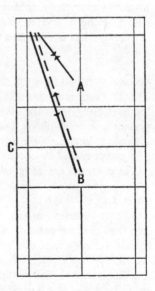

*Comment:* Sliced or flat drop.

109

FIG. 54
Forehand deep corner to opposite backhand net
corner. Shot down the line.

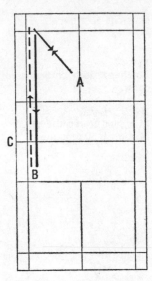

*Comment:* **A** can play a flat drop. He can use deception by beginning the movement for a sliced drop shot and then by turning racket face immediately prior to hitting the shuttle, he can play a reversed sliced drop. This is a very deceptive movement. In this sequence the player should master the flat drop before trying a reverse sliced drop shot, which is an advanced skill and requires perfect control and timing.

### COMMENTS ON DROP SHOT SEQUENCES
The nine sequences are all the possible combinations of drop shot returns. Taken simply they are easy to perform, but they become difficult under pressure. As the player becomes fatigued with the repetition, it is very difficult to maintain the fine touch quality needed to perform the stroke. The player begins to lose control and accuracy.

The practices are designed to strengthen these weaknesses.

### DROP SHOTS – FAST
The same sequences are used except **B** changes his base. A fast drop carries into the court a greater distance. **B** moves his position to a point behind the service line. **A**'s shot will be direct and downwards. The difference between the two types of stroke is that in the slow drop shots the shuttle travels higher and falls steeply as it loses speed. In the fast drop shot, the shuttle will travel in a straighter line keeping low over the net and carrying for a greater distance into the opposite court.

# DROP SHOT – COMBINATION SEQUENCES

## SEQUENCE 1

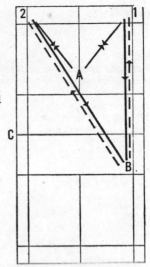

FIG. 55
Forehand overhead drop shot from backhand and forehand corners to opposite forehand net corner.

*Work Schedule*
Minimum 10 repetitions.
Maximum 40 repetitions.

*Comment:* **A** is under more pressure as he now has a two stroke sequence to perform and the shuttle only travels half the court distance each time. **B** should return the shuttle very high to allow **A** to move into position each time. This is important as correct positioning and balance by **A** is vital, if **A** is to achieve accuracy and control.

## SEQUENCE 2

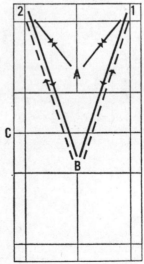

FIG. 56
Forehand overhead drop shot from forehand and backhand corners to opposite centre net area.

*Work Schedule*
Minimum 10 repetitions.
Maximum 40 repetitions.

*Comment:* Perform as in the previous sequence.

111

SEQUENCE 3

FIG. 57
Forehand overhead drop shot from forehand and
backhand corner to opposite net backhand corner.

*Work Schedule*
Minimum 10 repetitions.
Maximum 40 repetitions.

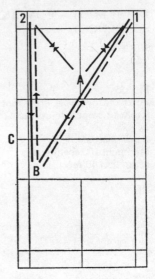

Comment: Perform as in previous sequence.

112

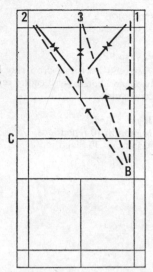

FIG. 58
Forehand overhead drop shot from backhand corner, centre rear court, and forehand corner to opposite forehand net corner.

*Work Schedule*
Minimum 10 repetitions.
Maximum 30 repetitions.

*Comment:*

(1) **A** is under continual pressure. The travel time is reduced as the shuttle only covers half court distance. To assist **A**, **B** should allow shuttle to drop near the floor before he returns it to **A**.

(2) Order of sequence develops footwork pattern. **A** covers a wide angle change of direction from 1 – 2 and two narrow angles from 2 – 3 and 3 – 1. This involves quick agile footwork to change direction from forwards to backwards.

(3) Though the pressure on **A** is very intense, he should at all times return to his centre. At first the centre may be established nearer to the rear court to allow **A** more time, but as soon as possible **A** should strive to reach the correct centre as shown in the diagram.

113

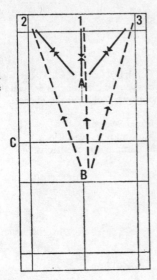

FIG. 59
Forehand overhead drop shot from forehand and backhand corner, and centre rear court to opposite centre net.

*Work Schedule*
Minimum 10 repetitions.
Maximum 30 repetitions.

*Comment:* Repeat as for previous sequence.
Keep to the order as shown. This is very important for developing precise footwork patterns.

SEQUENCE 6

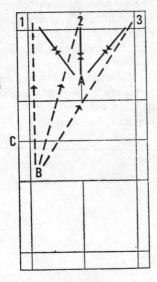

FIG. 60
Forehand overhead drop shots from forehand, backhand corners and centre rear court to opposite backhand net corner.

*Work Schedule*
Minimum 10 repetitions.
Maximum 30 repetitions.

*Comment:* Repeat as in previous sequence.
Keep to the correct order as shown.

## 26. TRAINING SEQUENCES

### (d) OVERHEAD BACKHAND CLEAR

This shot is usually only performed from the backhand side of the court and therefore the sequences are limited. There are certain body positions on arrival to the hitting area, which allow ease of stroke production. The comments on each sequence explain correct positioning. *It is important to read them carefully.*

The work schedule has been set with a minimum of 20 repetitions and a maximum of 100 repetitions. The player should begin with a target of 20 repetitions. As endurance and strength improves the number of repetitions to be performed in each sequence should be increased, until the player over a period of time is able to perform 100 repetitions before the onset of fatigue.

FIRST SEQUENCE

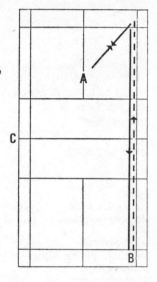

FIG. 61
Overhead backhand clear from backhand corner to opposite forehand corner.

*Work Schedule*
Minimum 20 repetitions.
Maximum 100 repetitions.

*Comment:* **A** will find that if he turns his back completely to the net, he will be able to perform this stroke down the line with accuracy and power. Accuracy is important as there is such a small margin of error in this particular sequence. By turning the back completely to the net, the natural line of the arm and racket will travel along that pathway. This positioning to allow the arm and racket to follow the natural line will apply in all backhand clear strokes. Under pressure the more skilled player may adapt this and achieve the chosen direction by using wrist deflection.

115

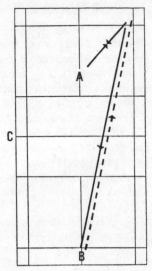

**FIG. 62**
Backhand corner to centre of opposite court. Repeat as in previous sequence.

*Work Schedule*
Minimum 20 repetitions.
Maximum 100 repetitions.

*Comment:* **A** should take a slightly open stance to strike shuttle along the correct pathway. **A** does not turn his back completely to the net, but instead his back faces **B** which gives him a more open stance in relation to the opposite court.

THIRD SEQUENCE

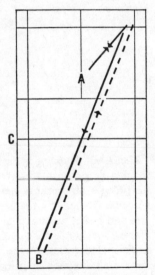

**FIG. 63**
Backhand corner to backhand corner along the diagonal. Repeat as in previous sequence.

*Work Schedule*
Minimum 20 repetitions.
Maximum 100 repetitions.

*Comment:* Difficult to perform. Requires good footwork and balance and perfect timing to send shuttle the full length of the diagonal.

## 27. TRAINING SEQUENCES
### (e) OVERHEAD BACKHAND DROP SHOT

As with previous drop shot sequences, the practices are designed for slow and fast drops. The feeder moves his receiving position according to the type of drop shot he will receive.

Strokes can be performed:
(a) flat
(b) sliced
(c) reverse sliced.

The last one (c) is very effective but difficult to perform as it requires perfect timing and awareness of the position of the racket face. The racket face moves as for a normal sliced drop and immediately prior to the impact, the angle of the racket face is altered by turning the head outwards. It is performed from the backhand court as though hitting a sliced cross-court drop shot and then reverse sliced down the line on a straight pathway. Very deceptive when performed correctly.

FIRST SEQUENCE

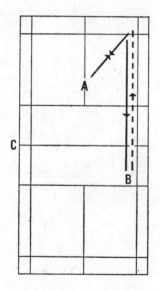

Fig. 64
Backhand corner to opposite forehand net corner.

*Work Schedule*
Minimum 10 repetitions.
Maximum 50 repetitions

*Comment:* Shuttle hit flat (open racket face) or with reversed slice. To allow **A** time to travel from centre to backhand corner **B** should hit the shuttle high. **A** must be perfectly balanced when playing the stroke and not be rushing back into position before the stroke is completed. The travelling from one position to another takes place during the time the shuttle is in the air.

117

SECOND SEQUENCE

## Fig. 65
Backhand corner to opposite centre net. Repeat as in previous sequence.

*Work Schedule*
Minimum 10 repetitions.
Maximum 50 repetitions.

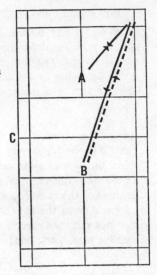

*Comment:* Sliced or flat stroke production.

THIRD SEQUENCE

## Fig. 66
Backhand corner to opposite backhand net corner.

*Work Schedule*
Minimum 10 repetitions.
Maximum 50 repetitions.

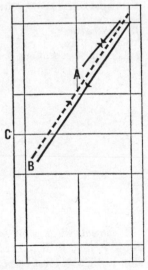

*Comment:* Sliced or hit flat. Usually the fast drop will be hit flat to bring it down quickly, though there is no set rule. The choice of stroke is left to the individual.

## 28. TRAINING SEQUENCES

### (f) COMBINATION OF STROKES

All the previous sequences have involved forehand and backhand clears: forehand and backhand drop shots: forehand and backhand return clears to drop shots. These have been set practices with the player being directed and having no alternative choice. Though there may be a risk of developing stereotyped play, the practices are justified by the need to develop strength in the game situation and perfect stroke production under pressure. All these sequences would be classed under the heading of 'Pressure Training'.

The next stage is to allow the player an alternative choice of return, which will be dependent on the situation he is in. The following sequences are designed to develop a combination of strokes and allow the player under pressure a variety of chosen returns.

FIG. 67
A returns all shots to diagonal corners of opponents court, i.e. backhand net corner and forehand deep corner.

Rally of 50 strokes.

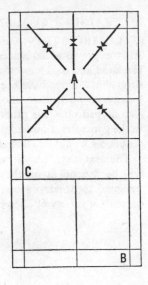

*Comment:* (1) **B** and **C** are in fixed positions. They may return the shuttle to either the three basic positions at rear of court (clears) or to the wide extremes at the net (drop shots).

(2) **A** must at all times return a drop shot to **C** or a clear to **B**. **A** can return a series of shots to the same area. He has a free choice in this. It is solely dependent on his situation and positioning.

**C** begins the rally by serving high to **A** and it continues until 50 consecutive strokes have been played. After 50 strokes the players change positions until each player has had a turn at being under pressure.

The aim of the sequence is to force **A** to run about under continued pressure and yet play shots of his own choice to two predetermined areas.

At all times **A** should return to his central position. The central position of **A** will vary slightly in each sequence. He may have to adjust his position to either side of the centre service line to narrow the angle of return.

If **A** makes a poor return to either **B** or **C**, they should move to return the shuttle to **A** and then quickly return to their fixed positions. Their position is the target for **A**; if they do not return to their position it is distracting to **A**, and upsets the aim of the sequence.

If the rally breaks down **C** begins again by serving high to **A** and the rally commences at the number of shots achieved before it broke down.

FIG. 68
**A** must return all shots to either backhand net
corner or backhand deep corner.

**Rally of 50 strokes.**

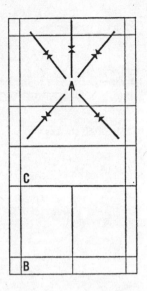

*Comment:* Perform as in the previous sequence.

FIG. 69
**A** returns all shots to diagonal corners of opponents
court, i.e. forehand net corner and backhand deep
corner.

**Rally of 50 strokes.**

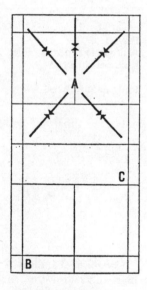

*Comment:* Perform as in first sequence.

121

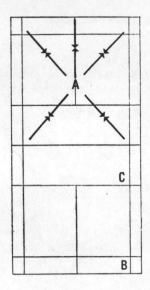

## FIG. 70
**A** returns all shots to forehand side of the opposite court, i.e. forehand net corner and forehand deep corner.

Rally of 50 strokes.

*Comment:* Perform as in first sequence.

FIFTH SEQUENCE

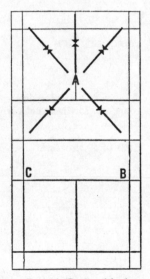

## FIG. 71
**A** drops to extremes of net, i.e. forehand and backhand net corners.

Rally of 50 strokes.

*Comment:* To allow **A** time to get into position **B** and **C** should clear high and return drop shots higher over the net than is usual in the game situation. The emphasis is not so much on **B** and **C** to make winning shots, but to make accurate placements and make **A** run about the court.

FIG. 72
**A** clears to extreme corners from any position, i.e. forehand and backhand deep corners.

Rally of 50 strokes.

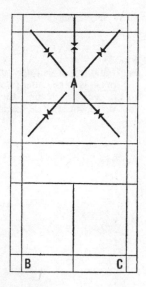

*Comment:* **B** and **C** can speed up or slow the rally down by sending high or low returns to **A**. This is performed according to the fitness of **A**.

## 29. TRAINING SEQUENCES

### (g) OVERHEAD BACKHAND SMASH

This is an extremely difficult stroke to perform with real power. It needs:

(a) Wrist strength.

(b) Perfect timing.

It is usually taken as a half court shot. It is a surprise stroke and relies on the element of surprise as a winning shot. It can be used with advantage from the rear court as a surprise tactical shot, accurately placed to force the opponent to hit upwards.

The sequences will be designed to improve the backhand smash as a tactical stroke rather than a winning stroke. At the same time the practices will improve the technical performance of the backhand smash and a strong player could easily develop the stroke into a winning smash.

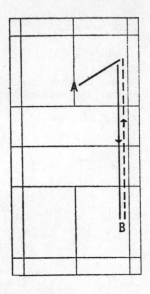

FIG. 73
Backhand smash – straight smash down the line. As the smash is to be under pressure **A** need not return to the centre each time, though he should turn to face opponent after each smash.

*Comment:* **B** has 10 shuttles (to save time if any are returned into the net). **B** feeds shuttle to **A**. **A** steps across and as he is hitting a straight smash down the line, he turns his back completely to the net. If the shot is returned accurately **A** moves round to face the net and **B** hits the shuttle back again. If the shot goes into the net **B** quickly feeds another shuttle to **A**. Thirty smashes and then **A** and **B** change positions.

FIG. 74
Backhand smash to centre. Repeat as in previous
sequence.

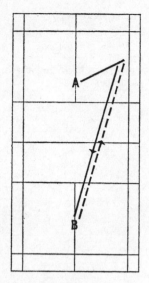

*Comment:* **A** has a slightly open stance to allow the pathway of racket
face to direct shuttle to centre. **A** need not turn his back completely to the
net, but rather facing towards **B**. This will place him in a position of a
slightly open stance in relation to the opposite court.

FIG. 75
Cross court backhand smash. Repeat as in previous
sequence.

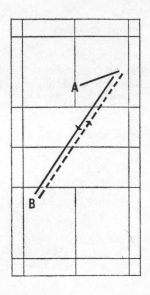

*Comment:* Used mainly in attacking a half-court shot and is almost a
smash drive. It would not be performed from the rear court as it would be
tactically a bad shot. **A** takes a more open position, almost facing the net
and slashes at the 'bird' to send it cross court. This is the winning type of
backhand smash.

## 30. TRAINING SEQUENCES

### (*h*) OVERHEAD FOREHAND SMASH

The big stroke in the game and one used for the outright winner. This can
be taken from anywhere in the court. Usually from the rear court it is advisable to smash straight or to the centre. From the half court it is possible
to smash cross court and win the point. Smashes can be aimed with a steep
angle or hit full length. They can be aimed at various points of the opponent's
body, or as tactical or strategic smashes to manoeuvre opponents round the
court to create an opening. However, this is dependent on the game skill of
the hitter. The object of these sequences is to build up power, strength and
stamina in smashing. The sequence will develop normal smashes and round-
the-head smashes. The latter requiring good footwork, balance and flexibility.

In the sequences which follow, if one player is to be placed under pressure,
he will be dependent on the feeder. It is necessary for the feeder to be able
to return smashes accurately. The feeder will be assisted by restricting the
placement area of the smash. Sometimes in combination play it will be
necessary to use two feeders.

126

On all sequences if **A** is unable to smash because of bad returns from **B**, **A** will send a high clear to **B** to keep the rally going. In these sequences the shuttle travels so fast that **A** cannot always return to the centre. However if **A** is able to get behind the shuttle quickly and smash into the shuttle, he will be able to travel forwards after his follow-through on the stroke.

FIRST SEQUENCE

FIG. 76
Forehand smash from forehand corner down the line (straight smash).

*Work Schedule*
50 smashes.

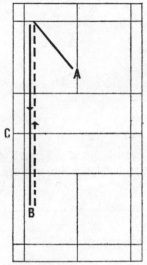

*Comment:* **B** feeds shuttle high to forehand corner of **A**. **A** hits straight smash, **B** returns high. If **B** unable to gain complete control and returns shot elsewhere to **A**, **A** returns a high clear to **B**, who then feeds shuttle to forehand of **A**.

Exercise lasts until **A** has performed 50 smashes. Players then change places.

**A** takes position of counter **C**.

**B** takes place of player **A**.

**C** takes place of feeder **B**.

127

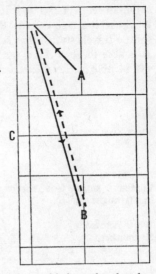

FIG. 77
Forehand smash from forehand corner to the centre.
Repeat as in previous sequence.

*Work Schedule*
50 smashes.

*Comment:* **A** must get body behind shuttle in order to hit into the shuttle. This will allow him to come forward to the centre position after each smash.

Fig. 78
Forehand smash – cross court. From forehand corner to opposite backhand side.

*Work Schedule*
50 smashes.

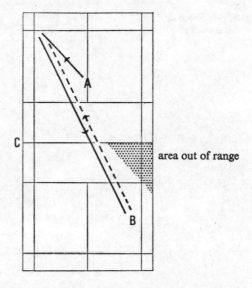

*Comment:* Very rarely used in doubles as it leaves a gap down opposite side of **A**'s court. However, it can be used in singles quite effectively.

FOURTH SEQUENCE

FIG. 79
Forehand smash from centre rear court to backhand
side of opposite court.

*Work Schedule*
50 smashes.

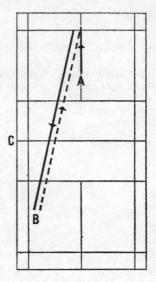

FIFTH SEQUENCE

FIG. 80
Centre to centre. Repeat as in previous sequence.

*Work Schedule*
50 smashes.

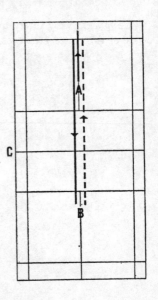

FIG. 81
Centre to forehand side of opposite court.

*Work Schedule*
50 smashes.

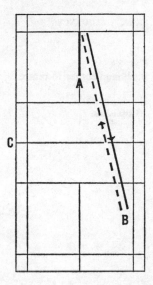

SEVENTH SEQUENCE

FIG. 82
Backhand corner to cross court.

*Work Schedule*
50 smashes.

out of range

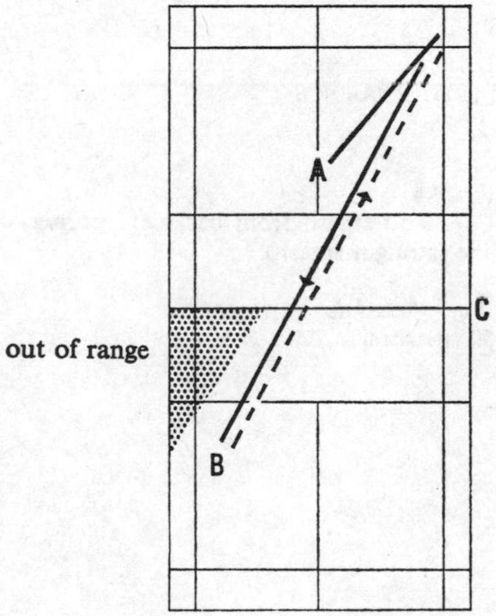

*Comment:* This is a smash which is very rarely used in doubles. In singles it can be effective as a surprise stroke. The shot is performed as a round-the-head smash, or if **A** can get behind the shuttle and in a sideways hitting position, it is performed as a normal smash directed cross-court.

131

EIGHTH SEQUENCE

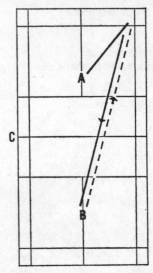

FIG. 83
Backhand corner to centre.

*Work Schedule*
50 smashes.

*Comment:* Performed as a round the head smash or a normal smash directed on the described pathway. Balance and footwork is very important.

NINTH SEQUENCE

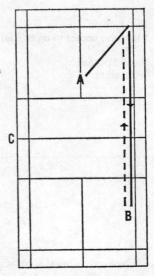

FIG. 84
Forehand smash from backhand corner down the line (straight smash).

*Work Schedule*
50 smashes.

*Comment:* Performed as a round-the-head smash or as a normal smash. Accuracy and control required as the smash down the line leaves little margin for error.

132

# 31. TRAINING SEQUENCES

## (i) COMBINATION SEQUENCE FOR SMASH AND RETURN OF SMASH

### (1) PRESSURE ON PLAYER SMASHING

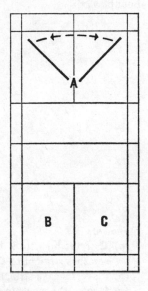

FIG. 85
Repeat until each player has performed 30 smashes.

**B** and **C** return the shuttle high to forehand and backhand side of rear court.
**A** smashes straight or cross court.

*Comment:* **A** must get feet behind shuttle each time in order to get weight into shot and be balanced.

**B** and **C** should clear high to give **A** more time between shots.

(2) SMASH AND RETURN OF SMASH

FIG. 86
Four players.

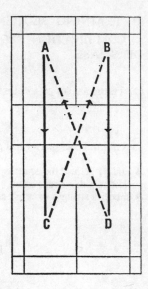

*Comment:*
   (a) **C** serves high to **B**. **B** smashes straight to **D**. **D** returns high to **A**. **A** smashes straight to **C**, etc.
   (b) Players smash straight. Receivers return cross court.
   (c) Controlled smashing to allow receivers to feed shuttle back more easily.
   (d) Play a rally of 60 strokes.
   (e) If the rally breaks down, **C** begins again with a high serve to **B**.

(3) SMASH AND RETURN OF SMASH

FIG. 87
Cross court smash. Straight return. Repeat as in
previous sequence.

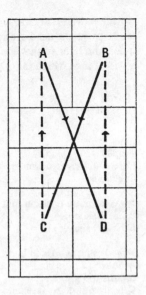

*Comment:* All players must try to be accurate with their placing of the
shuttle otherwise the rally tends to break down.

## 32. TRAINING SEQUENCES

### (j) FOREHAND AND BACKHAND DRIVES

Usually performed in half court play when shuttle is too low for an effective
smash and when player has to reach to the side for a shuttle. Drive can have
several pathways:

    (a) long flat drive

    (b) driving landing mid court and taken almost at bent arm smash height.

    Drives should keep low over the net, i.e. skim the net. It is usually a stroke
all good players can perform well. It is used with much effect in the Doubles
game.

USUAL FAULTS

    (1) Player goes back to take drive instead of stepping forwards into the
drive.

    (2) Player does not complete stroke and tends to move back to next
position too soon.

It is better, if possible, to move forward and across to drive and meet the
shuttle early. Balance is important in staying with shot until completion.

135

Many drives are taken too low because of bad footwork. The player tends to reach across and by doing so lowers his body. Steps should be quick and light so that the feet remain below body's centre of gravity and not a wide lunge which takes great leg strength to push off for next position.

FIRST SEQUENCE

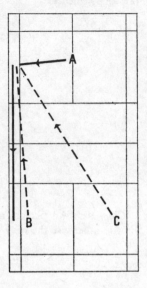

FIG. 88
Forehand drives down the line. Shuttles from two directions.

**A** takes centre position mid court.
**B** has 10 shuttles.
**C** has 10 shuttles.

**B** feeds shuttle to side line.
**A** moves across and drives straight, then quickly returns to base.
**C** feeds shuttle to forehand of **A** as soon as **A** has reached central position. Sequence continues until **B** and **C** have each fed **A** 10 shuttles.
Players move round until each has practised driving.

*Comment:* **A** has closed body position for straight driving.

136

FIG. 89
Forehand driving cross court. Shuttles from two
directions.

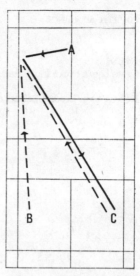

*Comment:* **A** has slightly more open body stance to allow hips to come
through and body to turn for cross court drive.

THIRD SEQUENCE

FIG. 90
Backhand drive down the line. Shuttle from two
directions.

Repeat as in Sequence 1.

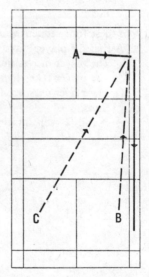

*Comment:* **A** has closed body position. Upper body twists to left on backswing. Back almost facing net.

FIG. 91
Cross court backhand drive.

Repeat as in Second Sequence.

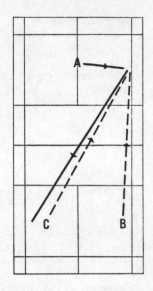

*Comment:* **A** has more open body position. Front foot offset to allow body to swing through freely.

In these four sequences on driving it is important:
(a) that the player stays with the shot until completion.
(b) The player moves quickly back to centre after completing the shot.
(c) The player takes light quick steps for good balance.
(d) The player uses open and closed positions for cross court and straight shots.
(e) **B** and **C** keep shuttles going without a stop.

# COMBINATION DRIVING SEQUENCE

FIFTH SEQUENCE

FIG. 92
Forehand and backhand strokes down the line.
Shuttles arriving on direct pathway.

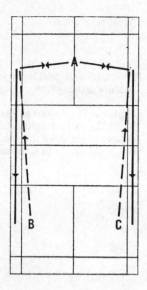

*Comment:* **A** central position. **B** feeds straight to **A**. **A** moves across and drives down the line and then returns to centre. **C** hits shuttle as soon as **A** has returned to centre. **A** moves across and hits backhand drive down the line and then returns to centre. **B** and **C** have 10 shuttles each. Sequence continues until shuttles used up.

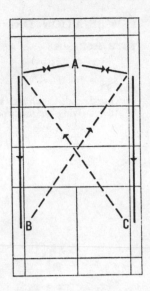

**FIG. 93**
Forehand and backhand strokes down the line.
Shuttles arriving from a diagonal pathway.

Repeat as in previous sequence.
**B** and **C** now feed shuttles on a diagonal pathway to
**A** who drives down the line.
**B** and **C** have 10 shuttles each.

*Comment:* **A**'s body position is closed for these two practices. He must still maintain light steps while moving and not lunge at shuttle. **B** and **C** must concentrate on their timing in feeding the shuttle.

SEVENTH SEQUENCE

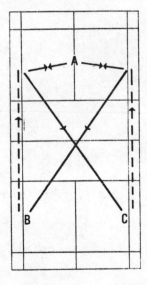

**FIG. 94**
Cross court forehand and backhand drives.

**A** receives shots on a direct pathway and drives them cross court.
**B** and **C** have 10 shuttles each.

EIGHTH SEQUENCE

Fig. 95
Cross court drives. Shuttle arriving from a cross
court direction.

B and C have 10 shuttles each.

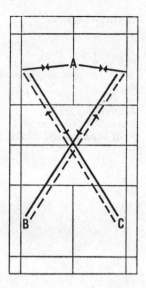

NINTH SEQUENCE

Fig. 96
Continuous rally – no feeding. A rallies against B
and C. Continuous driving.

A hits cross court.
B and C drive down the line.
A rally of 40 shots and then players move round one
place.
A plays forehand and backhand cross court.
B plays backhand straight.
C plays forehand straight.

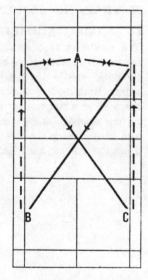

*Comment:* Each player has opportunity to play the four types of drive
during the sequence. Sequence puts A under continual pressure moving
from side to side, whilst B and C also gain practice in sending accurate
placements.

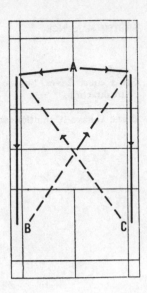

**FIG. 97**
As in previous sequence – continuous rally of 40 shots.

**A** hits down the line.
**B** and **C** hit cross court.
Rally begins with **C** feeding cross court shuttle to **A**.

## 33. TRAINING SEQUENCES

### (k) SERVING AND RECEIVING SERVICE

The following sequences are concerned with high flick serves and drive serves. Short serves have been omitted. This is because as the short serve is the basic serve in doubles, it has been included in the section on conditioned games. Both the high flick serve and the drive serve are doubles serves. They are used as a surprise serve and the emphasis in the following sequences is on the receiver, though the server gains practice in accurate serving. The aim is to develop the ability of the receiver in reacting quickly and making a positive reply to the high flick serve or the drive serve.

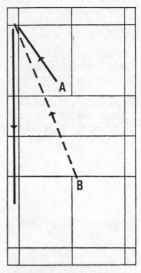

FIG. 98
**A** receiver.
**B** (20 shuttles). High flick service to forehand corner
of **A**.
**A** springs back and smashes down the line and then
returns to receiving position.
Change over after 20 smashes.

*Comment:* **A** must stand well up on service line when receiving.

**A** must get feet behind smash and be balanced so that follow through
takes him forward.

SECOND SEQUENCE

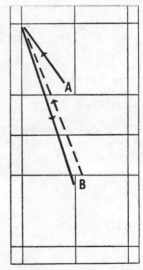

FIG. 99
Smash from forehand corner to centre.

Perform as in previous sequence.

*Comment:* For the smash to centre, **A** takes a slightly more open stance
during the actual smash.

**A** must stand well up to the line when receiving serve.

143

FIG. 100
Round-the-head smash from backhand corner of forehand court to centre.

(1) Repeat as in previous sequence except that **B** does flick serve to backhand of **A**.
(2) **A** springs back and performs round-the-head smash to the centre.

*Comment:* Requires flexibility in spine and shoulders as stance is side on to shuttle. An important practice for balance and footwork.

FOURTH SEQUENCE

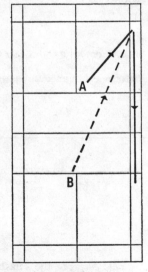

FIG. 101
Smash from backhand corner down the line.

20 serves each.

**B** serves high to backhand corner of **A**.
**A** moves back and does round-the-head smash down the line (straight).

*Comment:* Requires flexibility in spine and very good footwork.
Balance difficult to maintain if not performed with good body movement.

Fig. 102
Smash from backhand corner to centre.

20 serves each.

Repeat as in previous sequence.

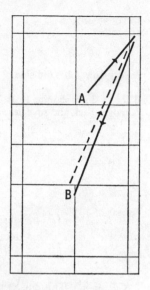

Comment: **A** does smash to centre. This is more round the head and directed to centre by:
(1) altering direction of racket face by wrist deflection
(2) getting behind shuttle and in line with flight of shuttle (this needs great speed).

FIG. 103
Smash from forehand side of backhand court.

**B** serves down the line to **A** forehand.
**A** moves back and smashes to centre.

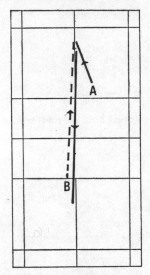

*Comments:* This smash is more difficult than it appears unless the receiver is aware of the subtle change of direction of his foot pattern and in the change of weight on his feet. The usual receiving stance of **A** places his feet in a line from the server to his backhand corner. His flow of movement will thus travel along this pathway.

On receiving this service, **A** from a stationary position along a set pathway must perform an abrupt change of direction to get backward and across on the open side (going against the natural movement of his shoulder girdle). The difficulty is quite simple to overcome if one is aware of it.

As **B** serves **A** reacts immediately to the usual high serve. His weight rocks back on the rear foot (the pathway taking him to the backhand corner). In this lies the difficulty in now getting across to the forehand side. His weight has travelled on to the rear foot and during the transition to the correct directional pathway, the shuttle has travelled a distance, and **A** finds difficulty in getting behind the shuttle. His usual answer is a smash back towards the retreating server or a drop shot return. Both these are performed because it is the easiest return in **A**'s unstable position. The server usually realises this without knowing why and waits for these possible returns to take advantage of them.

The correction for this difficulty of **A**'s is quite simple. It is a correction that ensures he can get his body behind the shuttle.

As **B** serves high, **A**, instead of rocking back on the rear foot and thus causing difficulty in the footwork transition, should be using his front leg to push off. Then as he is moving backwards, he can quickly place his rear leg to his right side and travel on the straight pathway. This will ensure that he does not waste time in the transition. These training sequences are designed for a smash return of service though other possible returns are attacking clears and drop shots. The smash is more effective as the server is still retreating and is therefore not completely balanced.

The serving side are usually able to retrieve the drop shot more easily from this set starting position than they are a smash. However this statement must be taken only as a general rule and not common in every situation.

## 34. TRAINING SEQUENCES

### (*l*) DRIVE SERVES

Drive serves are usually really effective when served to the backhand side of the receiver. Normal receiving stance is with the racket head up on the forehand side. Therefore a drive serve to the forehand requires a small movement (raising racket higher) to meet the serve. Receiving on the backhand side requires an arm action up and behind the head, with a quick twisting movement of the spine. This takes time, during which, the service becomes effective. It is easier to reply to it as a blocked drop shot return than a half or full smash, because of the time element.

The drive serve is not a common one as a surprise stroke, but players should be trained to meet it. Really the server gives his intention away because he must stand further back than normal to be able to perform the service without committing a service fault (i.e. lifting racket head).

FIRST SEQUENCE

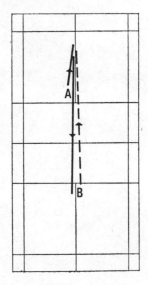

FIG. 104
Serve to backhand of **A**.

(1) **B** stands further back in court to serve otherwise danger of breaking service rule.
(2) **B** drives shuttle low across net to backhand of **A**.
(3) **A** steps back and either smashes or steers shuttle back across the net.
20 times and then change.

147

Fig. 105
Serve from backhand court to backhand of **A**.

20 serves.

**B** drives to backhand of **A**.
**A** steps back and across and smashes straight.

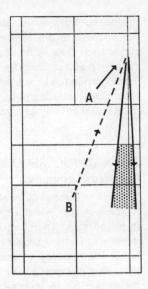

*Comment:* (1) Smash taken with arm action behind head or across front of face. (2) Serve is blocked for a drop shot return.

Fɪɢ. 106
Service from wide position in forehand court to
backhand of **A**.

**B** stands wide on forehand side.
**A** (I) normal stance; (2) backhand stance.
**A** returns by smashing down the centre (10 times)
**A** returns by dropping to opponent's backhand net
corner (10 times).

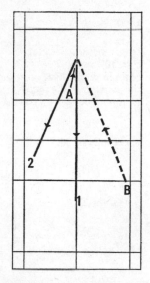

*Comment:* This serve is sometimes used to upset the rhythm of opponents.
It is easy to deal with if possible service returns have been practised and
experienced. Really it is a very weak service strategically as it leaves the
serving side in a weak defensive position. Often used, regretfully with good
effect.

## 35. TRAINING SEQUENCES

### (m) NET PLAY

There are two basic types of net play which occur during the game situation.

(1) A net situation in the forecourt which involves a drop shot rally, with
both sides trying to force a defensive shot and gain the attack.

(2) An attacking situation with the player in the forecourt waiting to
attack a poor return from a smash or attacking drop shot.

The following practice sequences are designed to quicken reflexes and
develop greater control. Several of the sequences are a standard practice,
others are learnt and improved in the normal game situation. However, by
isolating a situation from the game, and adding a competitive element in the
practice there should be an improvement in the ability of the player at the
net to meet possible situations.

Net play demands speed of movement, good footwork and perfect balance.
There is no allowance for error and great control is required for very fine
touch shots. It will help all players if they remember to watch the shuttle,
concentrate hard and keep the racket held high at all times between shots.

149

Fig. 107

Hairpin drops. This drop shot is named so because the pathway of the shuttle is similar to the shape of a hairpin. The shuttle travels close to the net in its flight.

A net rally of 30.

 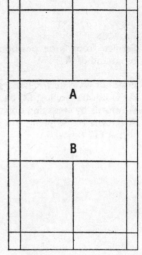

*Comment:* Each player to allow shuttle to drop near the floor. Play the stroke from floor level so that the shuttle 'climbs up and crawls over' the net.

Emphasis on balance, fine touch, control and accuracy. Though this type of rally is not a common one in the game, the situation does occur and it is easier to perform if the situation has been experienced and practised.

150

FIG. 108
Net rally. Meeting shuttle at top of net.

Practise for five minutes.

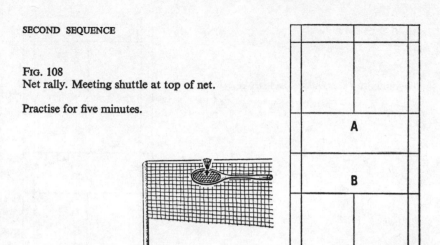

*Comment:* The aim is a net rally. Both players trying to meet shuttle as early as possible at top of net. This may not always be possible, but the emphasis should be to meet the shuttle at a high point. The practice is designed to develop fine touch, control and accuracy.

FIG. 109
Diagonal drop shots. Forehand stroke.

Rally of 30.

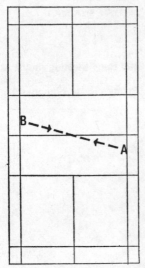

*Comment:* Stroke played (*a*) to out-position opponent; (*b*) if the shuttle is too close to the net to stroke vertically upwards.

Both players remain in the positions as shown in the diagram. The shuttle is hit from one to the other in a rally. The shuttle should keep very low when crossing the net.

FOURTH SEQUENCE

FIG. 110
Diagonal drop shot. Backhand stroke. Perform as in previous sequence.

Rally of 30.

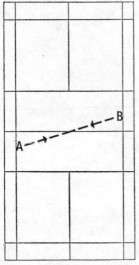

*Comment:* The emphasis is on developing control on the backhand side.

FIG. 111
Forehand and backhand net shots under pressure.

Rally of 20.

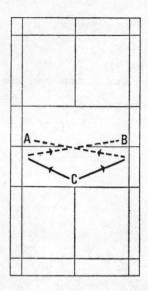

*Comment:* **C** plays drop to **A**. **A** performs straight drop. **C** returns diagonal drop to **B**. **B** returns straight drop. **C** plays diagonal drop to **A**, etc. **B** and **A** perform straight drops. **C** performs forehand and backhand diagonal drops under pressure. Rally of 20 and players change round until all have been placed in pressure situation.

FIG. 112
Vertical net shots under pressure.

Rally of 20 shots.

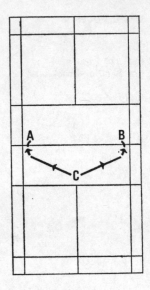

*Comment:* **A** and **B** play a diagonal drop shot. **C** plays a vertical drop shot in reply.

Players change positions after each rally. Perform as in the previous sequence.

FIG. 113
Net shot game. Game of 11 points.

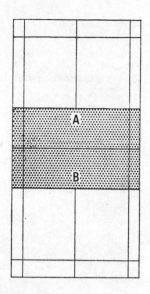

*Comment:* A net shot game in the forecourt (shaded area).
Play as normal singles except restricted to net shots.

Emphasis is on speed and control, fine touch, and deception in a competitive situation. The game is started by the server throwing the shuttle anywhere over the net into the forecourt. Server throws from the junction of the service line and the centre line.

FIG. 114
Drop shot or smash return to low drive.

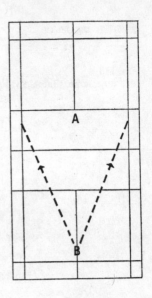

*Comment:* **A** takes up net position. **B** has 10 shuttles. **B** must drive a shuttle to skim the net past **A**.

**A** has to cut off drive by blocking with a drop shot or smashing down (keep score of successful attempts).

Element of surprise in that **B** can hit to either side of **A**. **A** must keep alert with racket up.

Players change positions after 10 drives.

FIG. 115
Net play attacking situation.

10 repetitions of situation.

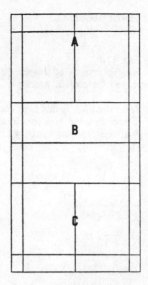

*Comment:* **C** has 10 shuttles. **C** hits high clear to **A**. **A** executes a controlled smash to **C** and **C** plays a low return of shot. **B** must attack return with drop shot or smash.

After 10 attempts players change round. Players to keep own score of successful attempts. This practice is dependent on all players being able to play their part. **A** must therefore be accurate with his smash. **C** must concentrate in order to play a successful return. **B** should keep alert to attack the return from from **C**.

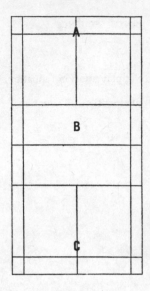

FIG. 116
Net return to a smash. 10 attempts each – keep
score of successful attempts.

A 10 shuttles. Sends high clear to C.
C smashes and attempts to smash past B.
B at net position must try to block the smash.

*Comment:* This situation would very rarely occur in a game. In fact it
would be bad positional play if it did. However, it is an excellent practice
for developing reflexes and control.


## 36. CONDITIONED GAMES

The idea behind a conditioned game is to emphasise and enforce that the
players are restricted to particular skills within the game. If accuracy and
control is required the game will be conditioned to bring out these factors.
This will also happen if the aim is to emphasise the smash or drop shot.
Main themes are to emphasise attack or defence, in which case the players
will be restricted to attacking strokes or defensive strokes, etc. There are
many varieties of conditioned games and in the next practices a few are
mentioned.

Games are conditioned for both singles and doubles.

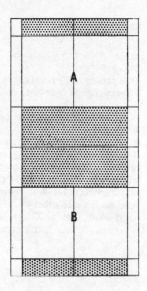

FIG. 117
Game of 21 points. Singles.
Each player is limited to drop shots and clears. The player must try to hit the shuttle in the shaded area. If the shuttle is hit into the free space the opposing player may allow it to drop to the ground, and win the point. If the player returns the shuttle instead of allowing it to drop the game will continue.
The idea behind this game is to emphasise accuracy in drop shots and good length in clears.

SMASH AND DROP

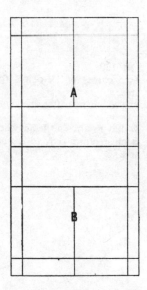

FIG. 118
Two games of 11 points.

A can only smash or drop.
B plays normal game. Change after one game.

*Comment:* **A** is forced to play attacking strokes throughout the game. **B** will never be forced to travel to the rear of his court to return the shuttle unless he has to move back to return a deep smash.

DROP SHOT GAME

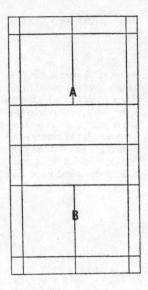

FIG. 119
Two games of 11 points.
Players change over after one game.

A can only drop shot (fast or slow).
B normal game.
A must be accurate or deceptive in his drop shot as
B knows what is coming each time. Unless A is
extremely accurate and deceptive with his strokes, he
will be placed in extremely difficult positions. It is
also important for A to return to his central singles
base each time, otherwise he will leave too much
court space free for B to return the shuttle. Fitness
is very important in this game.

RESTRICTED PLACEMENT AREA GAME

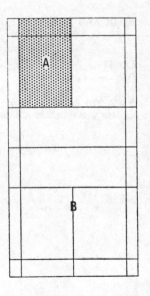

FIG. 120
Two games of 11 points (placement in forehand
area).
Players change after one game.

A may return shuttle anywhere.
B must return only to forehand side of A (shaded
area).

Comment: This game allows the player B under pressure a greater range
of possible returns. He may clear, smash, drive or drop shot, but is restricted
to only one area of the court.

160

RESTRICTED PLACEMENT AREA GAME

FIG. 121
Backhand area.
Two games of 11 points.
Players change over after one game.

A can return shuttle anywhere.
B must return shuttle only to backhand area of A
(shaded area).

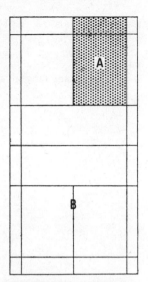

FRONT AND BACK GAME

FIG. 122
Two games of 11 points.
Players change after one game.

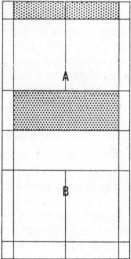

Comment: A returns anywhere.
B must return only to shaded area from whatever situation he is in.
B is restricted to drop shots and clears.
If B is accurate with these shots he is in a position to have an equal chance of winning. However, half court clears, etc., will allow A to dominate the game. The emphasis is on B to return accurate drop shots and good length strokes.

161

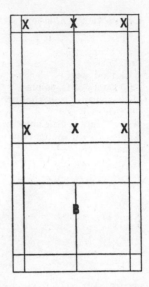

FIG. 123
Aim, accuracy and range of strokes.

**X = A**

*Comment:* **A** takes up set position and remains there for 5 minutes. **B** begins game by serving to **A** in his fixed position. **A** should try to make **B** run about the court.

**A** remains in a fixed spot and can return the shuttle anywhere, though he is not allowed to smash when at net position.

**B** must always return the shuttle to **A**.

**B** under great pressure in returning shuttle from any spot on court to a predetermined area.

As **B** can never win the game is played for 5 minutes then players change over.

The game is designed to develop the ability of the player under pressure to return the shuttle to a predetermined area from any position. This will require the ability to perform a wide range of shots from any situation. Fitness and ability to improvise are important for the player under pressure. It doesn't matter what type of stroke is played to return the shuttle to a given area, as long as the shuttle is returned accurately. It may require completely unorthodox strokes and awkward body movements. However two basic fundamentals are required, i.e. balance and control of the racket face.

The exercise is very demanding on the player and a high level of fitness is required, to maintain a long rally. The exercise will also improve fitness. The main emphasis is that **B** gets to every shot and is under continual pressure to do so. Because of the fixed return he becomes aware of the type of shot

162

necessary for return to a predetermined area from whatever situation he finds himself in. It is thus important that **B** returns to his central position after every stroke.

## CONDITIONED GAMES FOR DOUBLES

DEFENSIVE PLAY

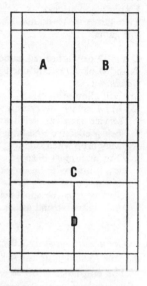

FIG. 124
Two games of 15 points.
Players change after one game.

**C** and **D** play a normal game.
**A** and **B** are conditioned, i.e.
(1) They must not smash.
(2) They must not drop shot unless playing a drop shot return to a drop shot.
(3) May play half court shots (steering shuttle but no driving).

*Comment:* The conditions at this level force **A** and **B** to play defensive Badminton throughout the game. They are really limited to defensive and attacking clears and the use of deception. In this type of game the important factor is to develop a sound defence. In order to win, everything must be returned and points will only be scored from the opponents' mistakes. The pair playing a normal game will have to penetrate the defence to win.

163

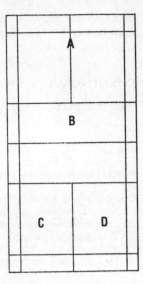

FIG. 125
Emphasis on attack.
Two games of 15 points. Players change over after
one game.

**C** and **D** play a normal game.
**A** and **B** play a conditioned game.
*Conditions*
(*a*) Not allowed to clear.
(*b*) Must smash everything when standing in the
service area, or drive and drop if shot taken
below effective smashing level.
(*c*) May drop when standing in rear court tramlines.
(*d*) Net man must push down everything above net
level, otherwise he drops to force opponents to
hit upwards.
(*e*) Service must be short service or flick service to
gain initiative and attack.

*Comment:* As **A** and **B** cannot clear shuttle high, **C** and **D** are not going to
be able to smash unless **A** and **B** play bad half court shots or poor drop shots.

The emphasis is on **A** and **B** to tighten up their half court game to gain
the attack, create openings and make the opportunity for a winning smash.

PART THREE

# Teaching Badminton

## 37. INTRODUCTION TO PART THREE

This Section of the book is written for anyone who wishes to teach Badminton. Considered in this category are:

(1) The teacher or physical education specialist in the school, who may or may not know anything about the game, yet wishes to introduce Badminton as an activity in the school physical education programme or as an extra-curricular School club activity.

(2) The leader of a youth club or boys' club, etc., who wishes to teach Badminton as a recreational activity for the club members.

(3) The Badminton club member, who would like to know how to teach other members to play the game, or to improve the performance of other club players.

(4) The club player, who holds a Coaching Award of the Badminton Association of England, and wishes to learn some new ideas and methods of teaching individuals and groups.

There are limits to how much information can be included in this section. The information is primarily concerned with introducing the game and teaching players to reach a competent standard of performance.

The ideas and methods presented are basic ones, which have been developed and proved successful over a number of years spent in teaching children in schools and young people in youth centres. This knowledge is presented for use and adaption by the teacher and the coach. Any further development will depend on the interest and the ability of the teacher and the coach.

The school is taken as the starting point, for it is the school which provides the source of the players of the future. If Badminton can be introduced to children in the school as an enjoyable active sport, then there is every reason for children to want to learn more about the game. Coaching groups of players, whether young children or adults, creates problems of organisation. Teaching the skills requires an ability to recognise basic faults, and a knowledge of how to correct them. For this reason many ideas are presented, which deal specifically with teaching the skills to large groups, and arranging those groups with regard to practising the skills. Further interest can be stimulated by introducing the element of competition in play. Games, matches and tournaments need to be organised to satisfy players of all standards. This has been considered and information provided in the organising of competitive play from the beginner level to an advanced level.

The teacher or the coach must use his knowledge and experience to select the material, which he decides is suitable for his needs.

## 38. TEACHING IN THE SCHOOL

As a sport, Badminton has much to offer children. The majority of secondary schoolchildren, even in the early years, discover that Badminton is quite an easy game to learn, and they derive a great deal of activity and enjoyment from playing. The racket is light to hold and the shuttle can be hit easily, without the need for much strength. At a very early stage in learning the game, children can play rallies and have simple forms of competitions amongst themselves.

It offers for the teacher an opportunity not only to provide the children with an enjoyable activity, involving the learning of skills, but also the opportunity to develop the child's social education. Badminton is a game played within a set framework of rules and regulations. It is a competitive game, which creates tensions due to the players' desire to win. It requires the use of fragile equipment, which if treated carelessly can easily be damaged. It requires standards of behaviour, which are established for the good of the game and for the development of healthy social relationships. For the teacher, there is the opportunity brought about by the nature of the game to teach children:

(1) To respect and conform to a set of rules.
(2) To respect and care for property.
(3) To acquire consideration for the other players in the game.
(4) To recognise and attain standards of dress and behaviour.

These factors are good social values, which can be related to the society in which the child lives. It is the teachers' role to make children aware of these values, and the game provides the opportunity to do so.

The game offers a great deal to the child who learns it. The opportunities to play Badminton after the school years are numerous. There are many Badminton clubs throughout the country and other centres where Badminton is played. It is an indoor game, and so is not affected by the weather. As a game which attracts a mixed membership, Badminton clubs are places which foster good mixed social relationships.

Overall, the game offers the boy or girl the opportunity to enjoy an active sport. After the school years it can be continued as a recreational sport, or for the keen players, as a highly skilled competitive sport.

## 39. PLANNING A PROGRAMME

Most schools are limited in the facilities available for playing Badminton. It is usually the case that there is only one gymnasium or large hall, which must be used for the normal P.E. lesson. As a result, Badminton is relegated to an extra-curricular activity, as a club activity for the senior boys and girls in the school. There are obvious practical difficulties in fitting it into the school P.E. curriculum. Even if it were possible to be introduced as a curriculum activity, the difficulty of providing a class of boys with enough activity to justify its inclusion can create doubts as to its value. Though twenty children on one court in a thirty or forty minute P.E. lesson provides its problems, it is possible to teach Badminton. However, for the sake of argument, we can presume that Badminton will be introduced as an activity in the school P.E. programme. It will either be included in the normal P.E. lesson, or the games lesson as an optional activity, or in the evening as an extra-curricular Club activity. The information which follows is a guide to the teacher regarding equipment and organising a large number of players on the one court.

## 40. EQUIPMENT AND FACILITIES

(1) The first requirement is a gymnasium or a large hall, in which a court must be marked out. The measurements can be taken from the Laws of the Game.

(2) Two Badminton posts and two nets. Always keep one net as a spare, in case one becomes torn and cannot be used. A good idea for the posts is to use multi-purpose bases and buy the posts separately. This saves money, and the bases can be used for other activities.

(3) *Rackets* – the ideal situation is to cater for a class of twenty players. This is possible on one court. Buy 20 average quality rackets and 20 presses. Rackets warp easily if not kept in a press when not in use. If twenty rackets are too expensive, a minimum of 10 rackets should be bought. This allows two players to share a racket. (They take turns during the practices).

(4) *Shuttlecocks* – Shuttlecocks are usually of the feathered type or the plastic type. The feathered ones are expensive and are damaged easily by beginners. The plastic shuttles are excellent for practice, though even these are damaged if not treated with care. If the school has matches, then feathered shuttles should be used. To begin with, order about six dozen plastic shuttles of various speeds, and a couple of dozen feathered shuttlecocks. A Sports shop will advise you on the price of shuttlecock suitable for your needs.

(5) *Care of Equipment* – All players should be taught from an early age to respect the equipment and handle it with care. The net should always be folded up after use, and the posts carried away and not dragged away. Rackets should be placed carefully in the presses and then held by the press when being carried. They should be stacked away neatly. Shuttlecocks should be collected and put away carefully in the container. During play most players have a habit of kicking shuttlecocks across the floor to their partner. Always insist upon the players picking up the shuttlecock to return it. If a player picks up a shuttlecock and hits it back to his partner, it is a chance to practise a stroke. This is a small point, but very relevant to learning the game.

## 41. INTRODUCING THE GAME

Children in the first year of the Secondary School are quite capable of learning to play Badminton. This may be at a simple level, but they have

169

no difficulty in learning to control the racket and hit the shuttle over the net. There is certainly no justification for the school of thought, which considers Badminton suitable only for the senior children. Unless, of course, the reason is one of numbers and facilities available. If the game is introduced in the daily P.E. curriculum, it will not be possible to teach the players to a very advanced standard. The lesson should be considered as an introductory one. The aim should be to give the children the opportunity to hit the shuttle with control, and to play simple rallies and games. The keener players should be given the chance to improve in an extra-curricular school club session.

The teacher need not be a player himself, if the children are to play at this level. The introductory lessons which follow are specially designed for a teacher to organise a class, and introduce Badminton, without any knowledge of the game. However, even for the teacher who is a competent player, the methods adopted for introducing Badminton are designed to suit the development of a beginner and have proved quite successful.

The following lessons are planned for a class of twenty children in a gymnasium or hall containing one badminton court. The average gymnasium or hall will accommodate a class this size if the lesson is well organised. With extra courts, more children can be accommodated, and the following plan may be used as a basis. If the class is larger than twenty, some children would have to take their turn to play. If problems of equipment and numbers beyond this occur, then the teacher can adapt the organisation of this basic plan to meet his requirements.

## 42. A PROGRAMME OF LESSONS

The aim of these lessons is to introduce Badminton to beginners. The beginners in this situation are considered to be schoolchildren. The age range may be from eleven years old in the first year of the Secondary school, to the teenagers in the final year of Secondary school. The methods employed in introducing Badminton may also be used for a beginner of any age, including adults.

The idea is that the teacher will establish set situations and present problems in which the children will explore the numerous possibilities there are of hitting the shuttlecock. In solving set problems, the children will gain a feeling for control of the racket; an appreciation of the varying flights of the shuttlecock; and an understanding of the factors involved in the movements required to hit a moving object over a net within the confinement of a particular floor area (i.e. the court). The teacher establishes the situation and presents the problem. The children explore, discover and learn for themselves.

170

# LESSON 1

FIG. 126

Players: X

Bench: ⟩

Rope: -----

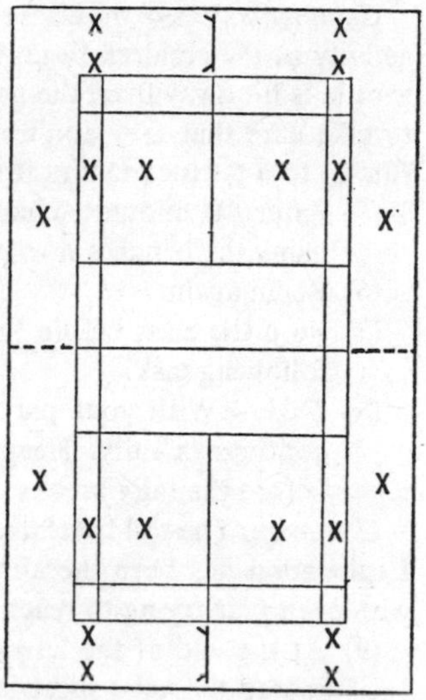

(A) ORGANISING THE LESSON

Lesson plan showing the organisation of class in the space available.

*The Court* – 8 players working in pairs. Each player opposite to his partner.

*Side of Court* – Rope or extra net or a bench, which continues from the court to divide the room.

4 players working in pairs.

*End of Court* – At each end the space is divided by a bench. 4 players at each end of the Court.

Players work in pairs.

Benches are used as beginners enjoy hitting the shuttle over some obstacle, i.e. rope, net, bench, etc. If one bench is too low, place another bench on top of the first bench.

Every player has a racket. The players work in pairs with one shuttle between them.

(B) TEACHING THE LESSON

*Aims* – To introduce Badminton and to explore ways of hitting the shuttle to a partner.

To acquire control of the racket.

To play a continuous rally.

(1) Give each player a racket.

(2) Organise the class into pairs and give each pair a shuttlecock.

(3) Space the class out in the positions as shown in the diagram.

(4) *Task* – With your partner, practise hitting the shuttle over the net to each other.

171

*Comments:* Leave the class to practise in this way. There will be tremendous activity as the children begin to play. Be on the lookout for collisions if the shuttle is hit away from the partner. After such an incident, remind the class to take care that they don't collide with anyone else. The task is to hit the shuttle to a partner so aim it towards the partner.

(5) After 10 minutes, change the class round. The children who were using the benches now change over with the children on the court.

(6) Begin again.

(7) Stop the class before the final ten minutes of the lesson and give the following task.

(8) *Task* – With your partner, try to hit the shuttle to each other in a continuous rally. Keep a score of the number of shots you make, before the rally breaks down; begin again.

*Comment:* The children have had plenty of practice without any instruction. Exploration has been the aim. Now the rallying takes a competitive form, with each pair trying to reach a target.

(9) At the end of the lesson, stop the class, and find out which pair has scored the most successful rally.

(10) Store equipment away. Make sure each child puts his racket in the press properly. Place the shuttles in the box, the base of the shuttle first. Show the class how to fold the net up neatly. Lift the posts and bases up to put them away, and the floor will not be marked. Insist upon standards of behaviour and care of equipment from the very beginning. After a while, this will become habit, and less time will be spent on preparing and storing equipment each lesson. This should apply to each lesson.

## LESSON 2

(A) ORGANISING THE LESSON

Organise the lesson as for Lesson 1.

(B) TEACHING THE LESSON

(1) First 5 minutes. Tell the class to practise rallying with a partner.

(2) Individual practice – give each player a shuttlecock. Give the following task.

(3) *Task* – Practise hitting the shuttle up in the air, making use of both sides of the racket. See how many times you can do this before the shuttle falls to the ground. Practise for 5 minutes.

*Comment:* The children learn control in hitting the shuttle upwards each time. To maintain a rally requires accuracy to hit the shuttle directly upwards.

(4) Return to the positions on court with your partner.

(5) *Task* – Practise different ways of hitting the shuttle to your partner,

172

making use of both sides of the racket. Try to find one grip for the front of the racket and one grip for the back of the racket.

*Comment:* The class now begins to experiment and explore different ways of hitting the shuttle. The change of grip leads up to forehand and backhand grips. For the moment, the players try to discover for themselves a grip which allows comfort and ease, when hitting the shuttle on different sides of the racket.

(6) Stop the class and change them round, i.e. benches to court, court to benches. Give a new task.

(7) *Task* – Now you have found several different ways of hitting the shuttle. Try to play a continuous rally with your partner, making use of the different ways whenever possible. Keep a count of the score.

*Comment:* There will be a wide variety of different ways, i.e. low shots, high shots, slow and fast shots, underarm and overhead shots, and forehand and backhand shots. Observe the class carefully. If you see a child making use of a variety of ways, stop the class and ask the player to demonstrate with his partner. This gives the class some new ideas.

(8) At the end of the task, stop and see which pair has scored the most successful rally.

(9) End of lesson and equipment is put away.


## LESSON 3

(A) ORGANISING THE LESSON

Organise the lesson as for Lessons 1 and 2.

(B) TEACHING THE LESSON

(1) Class practice for 5 minutes. Practise rallying with a partner, hitting the shuttle in different ways.

(2) Individual practice. Give each player a shuttlecock.

(3) *Task* – Practise on your own:

    (a) How softly can you hit the shuttle.

    (b) How high can you hit the shuttle.

    (c) Play a rally, using both sides of the racket, and show how softly you can hit the shuttle, and how high you can hit the shuttle.

*Comment:* Allow ten minutes for this practice. The emphasis is now on acquiring a 'feel' for the racket and learning control of the pace and flight of the shuttlecock.

(4) Return with your partner to your positions on court.

(5) *Task*

    (a) With your partner play a rally of soft shots.

    (b) Play a rally of high shots.

(c) Play a rally of both high and soft shots. Keep a count of your score.

*Comment:* The class are now beginning to learn control and different ways of hitting the shuttle. The rally is always made competitive to stimulate interest and motivate learning.

(6) After ten minutes, stop the class. See which pair has scored the most successful rally.

(7) Equipment away. End of Lesson.

## LESSON 4

(A) ORGANISING THE LESSON

(1) Organise the lessons as for the previous lessons.

(2) Partners – By now it will be obvious that there is a considerable range of ability among the class. Tell the class to select a partner who is about the same playing standard.

(B) TEACHING THE LESSON

(1) Allow five minutes rallying practice with the partner. Emphasise the need to show different ways of hitting the shuttle at different speeds i.e. soft shots and high shots.

(2) Stop the class and teach them the following skills:
The ready position
The forehand grip
The backhand grip
These are not difficult to demonstrate even for the teacher who is a non-player. The instructions for these skills can be read in the section on Learning Badminton. The class have already experimented with changing the grip when using different sides of the racket, so this should not be difficult for them.

(3) *Demonstration* – When demonstrating, always stand in such a position that every player can see the demonstration clearly. Demonstrate and explain. Demonstrate and tell the class to copy you. Go round the class and check carefully that each child has copied you correctly.

*Ready Position:*

(a) Space the class out so that every child can see you.

(b) Demonstrate from the front, facing the class.

(c) Demonstrate from the front, in a sideways position to the class.

(d) Tell the class to copy your position.

(e) Check that each child has copied you correctly.

(f) Give the practice for the ready position as described in the section Learning Badminton.

174

*Forehand Grip:*
(a) Demonstrate from the front of the class and face the class.
(b) Repeat the demonstration, slowly whilst the class copies the movement.
(c) Forehand grip is the 'shake hands' grip.
*Backhand Grip:*
Repeat as for the forehand grip. Backhand grip the thumb must be flat along the back of the handle of the racket.

Practise both these grips as described in the section Learning Badminton.

Teaching these skills should not take longer than ten minutes.

(4) *Individual Task*
Practise hitting the shuttle up in a continuous rally. Hit five shots, using the forehand grip, and five shots, using the backhand grip.

*Comment:* Whilst the class are practising, observe carefully and make sure that each individual is using both the correct forehand grip and the correct backhand grip.

(5) After five minutes, stop the class and tell them to practise with their partners.

(6) *Task* – Play a continuous rally with your partner. Use the forehand grip and the backhand grip when necessary. Keep a count of your score.

*Comment:* The children should use the forehand grip on the forehand side of the body and the backhand grip on the backhand side of the body. In between shots, each player should stand in the position of readiness. Observe closely and remind the players of this.

(7) Stop the class and check for the best rally score.

(8) End of lesson. Equipment is put away.


## LESSON 5

(A) ORGANISING THE LESSON
Repeat as for previous lessons.


(B) TEACHING THE LESSON
(1) Rallying practice with partner for five minutes. Class to use forehand and backhand grips and maintain an alert ready position between shots.

(2) *Individual task – 5 Minutes*
Practise hitting the shuttle high and low, using both forehand and backhand grips. Play a continuous rally and keep a count of your score.

*Comment:* The emphasis is on using the correct grip, control and accuracy.

(3) Stop class and check for the best score.

(4) Tell the class to prepare for partner work.

175

(5) *Task* – Play a continuous rally with your partner and use the forehand and backhand grip when necessary. If your first shot is a soft shot, your next one must be a high shot, i.e. soft, high, soft, high, etc. A soft shot drops just over the net. A high shot travels high to the back of the court.

*Comment:* The children are now placed in a situation where:
(a) they use both grips
(b) they must play high shots and soft shots (low shots)
(c) they play these shots from overhead positions and underarm positions.

(6) After ten minutes, change the players round. The players using the court change with the players using the end of the court.
(7) After another ten minutes, stop the class.
(8) End of lesson. Equipment is put away.


## LESSON 6

(A) ORGANISING THE LESSON

Repeat as for previous lessons.

(B) TEACHING THE LESSON

(1) Rallying practice with partner for five minutes, using the variety of methods so far learned. Begin the rally with an underarm shot to partner (this is the beginning of the serve in the game).
(2) After five minutes stop the class and give them a task.
(3) *Task* – Practise with your partner. When you hit the shuttle, find ways of moving to it so that when you hit it you can keep your feet perfectly still.

*Comment:* Two of the important factors in playing a stroke are footwork and balance. This task allows the class to discover for themselves different ways of using the feet with the intention of keeping the feet still and balanced during the stroke. Do not allow the players to avoid the task. Keep reminding them of it and insist upon stillness during the hitting phase. A coaching point to remember when observing the players is that to achieve stillness in a balanced position, the whole foot or feet must be planted completely on the ground to take the body weight. Look for this and select players who can do it to demonstrate.

(4) After ten minutes, change the class round. All players have a turn on the court and on the benches.
(5) For the first ten minutes give the rallying practice with each pair trying to score a high number of shots before the rally breaks down.
(6) Check the scores to discover the best pair.
(7) End of Lesson. Put equipment away.

The first six lessons have been concerned with learning to hit the shuttle in a variety of ways. The class has learned the ready position, the grip and explored different ways of moving and holding stillness during the stroke, i.e. footwork and balance. Interest has been stimulated by simple rallying competitions and solving the tasks set by the teacher. The class will now be requesting competitive games. At this stage, they are now ready for competitions on a simple level.

The following lessons are all concerned with practice and play in a competitive form.

## LESSON 7

### (A) ORGANISING THE LESSON

FIG. 127

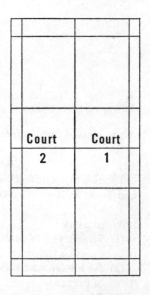

Divide the court into two equal lengths by drawing a line to connect the two centre service lines. (See diagram).

The court now contains two separate narrow singles courts, which will be used as such in all the following practices and games. The boundaries of each court are the centre line to the outer side line and the end lines.

(B) TEACHING THE LESSON

(1) TEAM ROTATION RALLY

FIG. 128

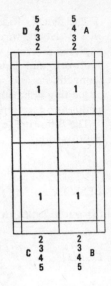

The class is divided into 4 equal teams.

Teams **A, B, C, D**

**A** versus **B**       **C** versus **D**

The following instructions for Team **A** and Team **B** also apply to Team **C** and Team **D**. This practice is played for the first half of the lesson.

HOW TO PLAY

(1) The players of each team are numbered in order from one to five. **A1** occupies the centre of the court and **B1** occupies the centre of the court.

(2) **A1** hits an underarm shot to **B1** and then **A1** runs quickly to the rear of his team.

(3) **B1** hits the shuttle back as **A2** runs on court to play his shot.

(4) **B1** runs off court as **B2** takes his place.

Play continues in this way with each team keeping a score of the number of shots played before the rally breaks down.

(5) If the rally breaks down, it begins with a serve from the player whose turn it is to hit the shuttle.

(6) At the end of fifteen minutes, stop the game and check which 2 teams have scored the most successful rally, i.e. **A** and **B** or **C** and **D**.

178

## (2) INDIVIDUAL ROTATION RALLY

Fig. 129

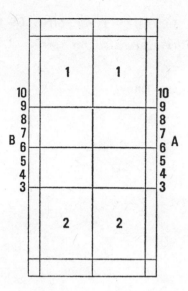

HOW TO PLAY

(1) The players are divided into 2 groups.

(2) The players in each group are numbered from one to ten.

(3) Each group occupies a singles court.

(4) The instructions for Group **A** also apply to Group **B**.

(5) **A1** and **A2** occupy the court.

(6) **A1** hits an underarm shot to **A2** and a rally commences.

(7) The first player to make a mistake goes off court and the next player in order takes his place on court.

(8) If a player does not make a mistake he stays on court all the time. If a player makes a mistake he goes off court to the end of the queue and the next player takes his place.

*Comments:* Both these practices stimulate interest and the players are very enthusiastic about the practice. The aims of the lesson are to promote learning in a competitive situation and provide enjoyment and activity.

179

# LESSON 8  TEAM SINGLES COMPETITION

(A) ORGANISING THE LESSON

FIG. 130

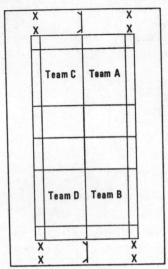

The lesson is organised for competitive singles between two teams

Team **A** versus Team **B**

Team **C** versus Team **D**

Benches are provided at the ends of the court for players to practise whilst waiting to go on court. The idea is always to provide activity.

HOW TO PLAY

(1) The instructions for Team **A** versus Team **B** also apply to Teams **C** and **D**.

(2) The players in each team are numbered from one to five in order.

(3) Each player plays in turn a member of the opposite team.

(4) A game is up to five points. The players toss for service. The server must hit an underarm shot so that the shuttle crosses the front service line and lands in the opposite court to be good. Only the server can add points to his score. If he loses the serve, his opponent wins the serve and can add points to his score. To win a point, hit the shuttle to the ground in the opponent's court.

(5) The order of play is as follows:

| Team **A** | – | Team **B** |
|:---:|:---:|:---:|
| 1 | v | 1 |
| 2 | v | 2 |
| 3 | v | 3 |

180

| | | |
|---|---|---|
| 4 | v | 4 |
| 5 | v | 5 |

| | | |
|---|---|---|
| 1 | v | 2 |
| 2 | v | 3 |
| 3 | v | 4 |
| 4 | v | 5 |
| 5 | v | 1 |

| | | |
|---|---|---|
| 1 | v | 3 |
| 2 | v | 4 |
| 3 | v | 5 |
| 4 | v | 1 |
| 5 | v | 2 |

| | | |
|---|---|---|
| 1 | v | 4 |
| 2 | v | 5 |
| 3 | v | 1 |
| 4 | v | 2 |
| 5 | v | 3 |

| | | |
|---|---|---|
| 1 | v | 5 |
| 2 | v | 1 |
| 3 | v | 2 |
| 4 | v | 3 |
| 5 | v | 4 |

(6) The score is recorded in the order of play, viz.

| | A | v | B | |
|---|---|---|---|---|
| L | 1 | ------ v ------ | 1 | W |
| W | 2 | ------ v ------ | 2 | L |
| W | 3 | ------ v ------ | 3 | L |
| L | 4 | ------ v ------ | 4 | W |
| W | 5 | ------ v ------ | 5 | L |

(7) At the end of play, or the end of the lesson, add up the total wins and losses for each team, to decide the winner.


## LESSON 9 TEAM SINGLES COMPETITION

The lesson is the same as the previous lesson.

The two winning teams of the previous lesson play for the Team Singles Championship. The two losing teams play for third and fourth place.

*Comments:* This type of lesson arouses tremendous enthusiasm amongst the children. Each player is now playing a competitive singles match where the emphasis is on winning. The children also begin to grasp the system of scoring and serving into a predetermined area.


## LESSON 10

ORGANISATION OF LESSON

Organise the lesson as for Lesson 1.

TEACHING THE LESSON

(1) The class work in pairs on rallying practice.
(2) After fifteen minutes the players change over, i.e. court to benches, benches to court.
(3) For each half of the lesson give the following task.
(4) *Task* – Practise rallying with your partner. Use the forehand and backhand grip and see how many ways you can hit the shuttle using these grips.

*Comment:* During this series of lessons the children have explored the numerous possibilities of hitting the shuttlecock. This has been developed further in competitive play with the accent on winning. When the emphasis is on winning, the children try harder and are more determined in their efforts. Usually at this level there is an improvement in the ability to move to the shuttle and play a shot. This final introductory lesson returns to the simple rallying practice. It will be noted that the scores increase quite considerably after having played competitive games.


SUMMARY

This series of ten introductory lessons are enough for any class of beginners. In the school situation they cover about a term's work. They are basic lessons, which have been devised for beginners and proved to be successful.

The ideas may be adapted, but any alterations are left to the individual teacher.

The beginner is now ready for the next phase, which is applicable to both schools and adult Badminton clubs.

If the non-playing teacher wishes to use the methods which follow, he will need to acquire more knowledge about the game. The emphasis is now on coaching the skills and tactics to a group of players.

## 43. TEACHING THE STROKES

ANALYSING THE STROKES

Once the player has reached the stage when he can hit the shuttle from a low position or an overhead position, and play a continuous rally, he is ready to learn the skills of the game. The role of the coach is to teach the skills in the game and the basic tactics required to play the game.

The requirements of a coach are:

(1) Knowledge of the game.
(2) Knowledge of the skills and tactics.
(3) Ability to recognise faults and correct faults.
(4) Ability to demonstrate a skill correctly.
(5) Ability to organise groups and provide enjoyable activity in the learning situation.

The strokes will be analysed under the following headings:

(1) Position of readiness.
(2) Grip.
(3) Footwork and balance.
(4) Preparation.
(5) Action.
(6) Recovery.

Each stroke has been explained fully in the section on 'Learning Badminton'. The coach can refer to this section to discover the correct method for any particular stroke. Once this knowledge has been learned and understood, the coach must be able to recognise faults in stroke production and to correct the faults.

If each stroke is analysed under the heading of position of readiness, grip, footwork and balance, preparation, action and recovery, there should be no difficulty in analysing a stroke, recognising the fault and correcting the fault.

Each stroke involves a complete cycle of movement.

The player stands ready. As the shuttle approaches, he takes up the correct grip (forehand or backhand grip). He moves quickly to the hitting position and then stops. This involves correct footwork and good balance. Once in position, he prepares to hit the shuttle (preparation and backswing). He hits the shuttle, the hitting action. After impact the racket follows through as the player recovers in a balanced position. The player returns to his position of readiness.

183

If the stroke is badly performed, the coach quickly analyses each stage until he decides which stage was wrong.

## EXAMPLES

(1) STROKE – OVERHEAD FOREHAND CLEAR

*Analysis by coach:*

| | |
|---|---|
| Ready position | – Correct |
| Grip | – Correct |
| Footwork | – Slow |
| Balance | – Slightly off balance |
| Preparation | – Hurried |
| Action | – Late |
| Recovery | – Snatched |

The player has moved for a stroke, arrived late and had to make a quick attempt at hitting the shuttle. From the above analysis the coach sees that slow footwork has affected the whole stroke, with a gradual deterioration of each phase of the stroke.

The coach would correct this fault by giving footwork practice to quicken the player's feet movements.

(2) STROKE – OVERHEAD FOREHAND SMASH

The player smashes the shuttle on a horizontal level and not downwards.

*Analysis by coach:*

| | |
|---|---|
| Ready position | – Correct |
| Grip | – Correct |
| Footwork | – Correct |
| Balance | – Correct |
| Preparation | – Correct |
| Action | – Bent arm, push not throw |
| Recovery | – Wrong |

From his analysis the coach decides that the player went wrong in the action phase. The correct action is to throw upwards at full arm stretch, and allow the wrist to whip the racket head over the top of the shuttle. The shuttle is hit downwards.

The player's action involved a bent arm. This is usually caused by dropping the elbow and pushing at the shuttle instead of throwing at it.

The correction is for the coach to decide, but will involve an upward throwing action to full arm stretch.

It is not possible to mention every fault and every correction. Use this method of analysing strokes, and with practice and experience, the ability to observe and analyse movements will improve. The important factor in coaching is an understanding of the principles involved in hitting the shuttle. This method of analysing will be quite helpful to begin with.

Coaching the strokes to a group of players creates problems of organisation. The players may vary in ability and numbers. The size of the playing space may also vary. Whatever the situation, the coach must organise the players so that all learn the stroke and all have the opportunity to practise the stroke.

When coaching any stroke, the coach should demonstrate to give the players an opportunity of observing the correct action. The coach should explain what the stroke is and when it is used. He must give the class the opportunity to copy the stroke and practise the stroke. During the copying and practising phase, the coach can observe the class and correct any faults which occur.

DEMONSTRATION AND EXPLANATION
For all strokes. Space the class out in the room, so that every player is able to:
(a) see the demonstration clearly
(b) hear the explanation
(c) copy the stroke freely without colliding with another player.

The best position is for the class to be at the side on which the particular arm action is being demonstrated.

When the class is in position to see the stroke clearly, demonstrate the correct stroke several times with an explanation of the movements involved.

SHADOWING
Allow the class to shadow your movements slowly as you demonstrate each stage from the ready position, i.e. footwork, balance, preparation, action and recovery. As soon as possible join these strokes together in a continuous sequence of movement. The player begins to feel the rhythm of the movement and the movement sensation of his actions.

PRACTICE
Place the class in positions on court to practise the stroke and hit the shuttle. Whilst they are working, observe carefully and correct any faults which occur.

## ORGANISING GROUPS FOR STROKE PRACTICES
The most difficult task of the coach is to organise his class in a restricted area, i.e. the court. All the players must be kept occupied practising the various strokes.

The basic type of practice is the isolated stroke practice involving a feeder and a player or several players. The feeder must hit the shuttle accurately for the player to perform the stroke being learned. The practice is isolated as the player performs one stroke and then positions himself to wait for the feeder to hit another shuttle to him. The play is not continuous. The feeder may also feed by hand, i.e. to ensure accurate feeding in the early stages, the feeder may throw the shuttle to the player.

ISOLATED STROKE PRACTICE

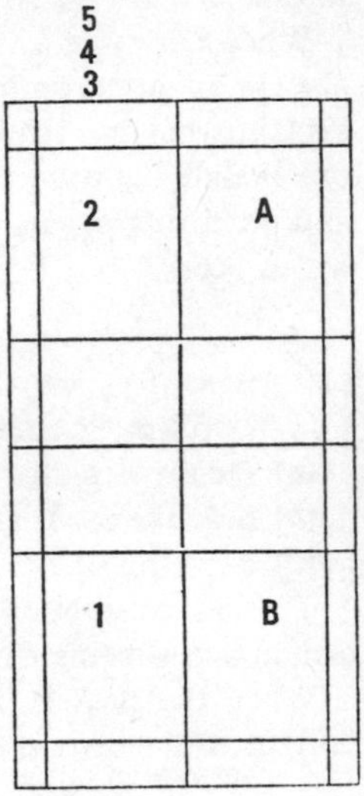

FIG. 131
The court is divided into two separate sections lengthways.

**B** is the feeder.
**A** is the player practising the stroke.
For example – the overhead forehand drop shot.
**B** hits a shuttle high to **A**. **A** is in the position of readiness. He moves, balances, prepares, hits the shuttle and recovers. **B** allows the shuttle to drop to the floor. **B** picks up the shuttle and hits another high one to **A**, etc.

Another method as illustrated:
**I** serves a high shuttle to **2**. **2** plays an overhead dropshot and goes off court.
**3** takes up his position and **I** hits the shuttle to **3** who plays his stroke. When all the players have had a turn **I** changes over to practise and **2** takes the turn of feeder.

This sort of practice can be applied to any stroke, and many variations devised.

The following practices are concerned mainly with a group of players performing strokes in a continuous rally.

186

# 44. GROUP STROKE PRACTICES

PRACTICE 1: OVERHEAD FOREHAND CLEAR

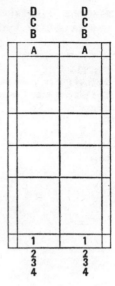

FIG. 132

*16 players*
The players stand in the positions as shown.

The court is divided into two equal lengths. Two groups of players are in each separate court.

ORDER OF PLAY
**A** hits the shuttle high to **I**.
**I** clears the shuttle back high to **B**.
**B** clears to **2**.
**2** clears to **C**.
**C** clears to **3**.
**3** clears to **D**.
**D** clears to **4**.
**4** clears to **A**.
**A** clears to **I**.
The sequence is repeated continuously until the rally breaks down. The players keep a score of the number of continuous shots achieved before the rally breaks down.

*Comment:* This practice emphasises the overhead forehand clear for a large group of players. The coach should encourage the players to maintain the rally. During the rally the coach has the opportunity to correct the players' stroke production.

187

PRACTICE 2: OVERHEAD FOREHAND DROP SHOT; UNDERARM LOW RETURN; UNDERARM CLEAR

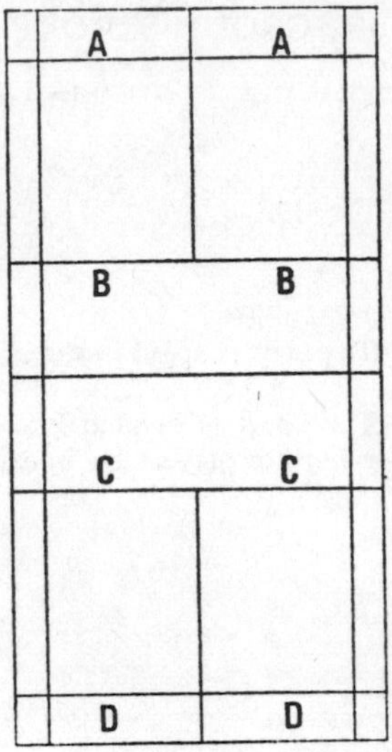


FIG. 133
*8 players*
The players stand in the positions as shown in the diagram.

The court is divided down the middle into two equal lengths. Four players occupy each section of the court.

ORDER OF PLAY

The rally begins with **C** who hits an underarm clear to **A**.

**A** hits an overhead forehand drop shot to **C**.

**C** hits an underarm low return to **B**.

**B** hits an underarm clear to **D**.

**D** hits an overhead forehand drop shot to **B**.

**B** hits an underarm low return to **C**.

**C** hits an underarm clear to **A**.

The cycle begins again. After ten repetitions **A** and **D** change over with **B** and **C**.

*Comment:* Each player must concentrate on his order in the sequence. **B** and **C** play alternately underarm low returns and underarm clears. If the sequence breaks down, **C** starts it again with an underarm clear to **A**. During this session the coach should observe and correct faults as they occur.

PRACTICE 3: OVERHEAD FOREHAND CLEAR;
OVERHEAD FOREHAND DROP SHOT; UNDERARM
LOW RETURN

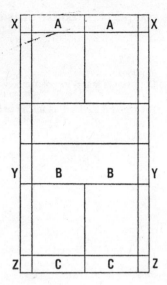

FIG. 134
*12 players*
The players stand in the positions as shown.

ORDER OF PLAY
(1) **B** hits an underarm clear to **A**.
    **A** hits an overhead forehand clear to **C**.
    **C** hits an overhead forehand clear to **A**.
    **A** hits an overhead forehand drop shot to **B**.
    **B** hits an underarm clear to **A**.
    This is one sequence. Repeat for ten repetitions.
(2) **X**, **Y** and **Z** change with **A**, **B** and **C** for ten repetitions.
(3) **A**, **B** and **C** change with **X**, **Y** and **Z**.
    Then the players move round one place on court.
    **C** to **B**     **B** to **A**     **A** to **C**.
    Repeat the sequence for ten repetitions.
(4) **A**, **B** and **C** come off the court and **X**, **Y** and **Z** go on court.
    **X**, **Y** and **Z** move round one place.
    **Z** to **Y**     **Y** to **X**     **X** to **Z**.
    Repeat the sequence for ten repetitions.
(5) This procedure is continued until all the players have had a turn in
    each position.
*Comments:* The players must concentrate to keep the rally going. The
coach should observe and correct faults as they occur.

FIG. 135
*16 players*
The players stand in positions as shown.

The court is divided as in the previous practice.

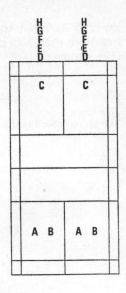

ORDER OF PLAY
A and B have a dozen shuttles.
A serves high to C.
C plays an overhead forehand smash.
B immediately serves high as C finishes his smash.
C has to repeat the smash.
Each player takes a turn to smash a shuttle twice in quick succession.
When all the players have had a turn C and D take the place of A and B and the practice is repeated.

*Comment:* The emphasis is on a quick recovery after a smash, to be ready to perform a second smash. The coach should observe and correct faults. He should make sure that the feeders A and B serve the shuttle accurately with correct timing between the two smashes.

190

PRACTICE 5: OVERHEAD FOREHAND SMASH;
UNDERARM LOW RETURN FROM FOREHAND
SIDE; UNDERARM CLEAR

FIG. 136
*6 players*
The players stand in the positions as shown in the
diagram.

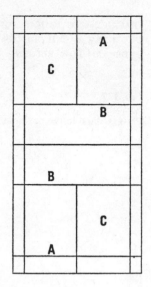

ORDER OF PLAY

**C** serves underarm clear to **A**.

**A** plays an overhead forehand smash to **C**.

**C** hits an underarm forehand low return to **B**.

**B** hits an underarm low return to **C**.

**C** hits an underarm clear to **A**.

The sequence is repeated for ten repetitions.

After ten repetitions the players move round one place.

**C** to **B**    **B** to **A**    **A** to **C**.

This is repeated until each player has a turn in each position.

*Comment:* The emphasis is on smashing and particularly the return of the smash. The player receiving the smash must slow the shuttle down to play an underarm forehand low return to the player near the net. The smash should be hit straight down the side line to the player receiving the smash.

191

PRACTICE 6: OVERHEAD FOREHAND SMASH;
UNDERARM BACKHAND LOW RETURN;
UNDERARM LOW RETURN

FIG. 137
*6 players*
Players stand in the positions as shown.

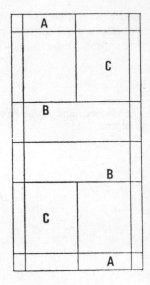

ORDER OF PLAY

C hits an underarm clear to A.

A smashes down the line to the backhand side of C.

C hits an underarm backhand low return to B.

B hits an underarm low return to C.

C hits an underarm clear to A.

The sequence is repeated for 10 repetitions.

The players move round after each series of 10 repetitions until all have a turn in each position.

*Comment:* The emphasis is on the smash and an underarm backhand low return to the smash.

192

PRACTICE 7: OVERHEAD FOREHAND SMASH;
UNDERARM LOW RETURN; DAB SHOT FROM
THE NET.

FIG. 138
*6 players*
The players stand in the positions as shown.

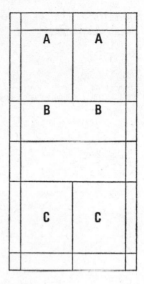

ORDER OF PLAY
  C serves an underarm clear to **A**.
  **A** hits an overhead forehand smash to **C**.
  **C** hits an underarm low return to **B**.
  **B** steps forward and plays a dab shot to hit the shuttle to the floor as it crosses the net.
  This is one sequence.
  Repeat for 10 repetitions.
  After each 10 repetitions, the player moves round until each player has a turn in each position.

193

PRACTICE 8: OVERHEAD FOREHAND SMASH;
UNDERARM CLEAR

FIG. 139
*16 players*
The players stand in the positions as shown.

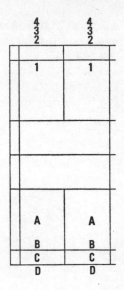

ORDER OF PLAY

A serves high to I and moves away to the end of the line.
I smashes to B.
B clears to 2.
2 smashes to C.
C clears to 3.
3 smashes to D.
D clears to 4.
4 smashes to A.
A clears to I and the sequence is repeated 10 times.
After 10 repetitions the players change over.

*Comment:* It is difficult to maintain a continuous rally in this way. Th
coach should insist that the players hit controlled smashes and aim fo
accuracy in placement for the receiver to clear.

SUMMARY

The emphasis in these eight practices has been on forehand strokes. Th
practices may be repeated with the emphasis on backhand strokes. Thes
are a few basic ideas.

The basic idea has been to accommodate a group of players on one cour
Any method which provides purposeful activity for a group of players o
the court is justified for inclusion in a practice session.

194

## 45. COACHING TACTICS

The intention is to coach players in Doubles tactics. The tactics under discussion are restricted to the service positions and the first moves after the service. Most beginners find it extremely difficult to position themselves after the service. This is important as the development of the play after the serve involves gaining the attack or being placed on the defensive. After this stage, the play opens up and the usual basic tactics are employed. These may be referred to in the section on 'Learning Badminton'.

In all the following progressions, the coach should explain clearly the intention of the practice. The players are restricted to the movements described in each stage of the development of tactics, based on a short serve and a high serve.

## DOUBLES TACTICS
## DEVELOPMENT BASED ON A SHORT SERVE

STAGE 1: TO SERVE SHORT AND MOVE IN AFTER
THE SERVE

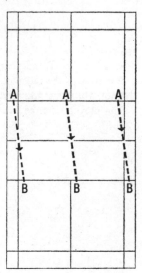

FIG. 140
*6 players*
Players must practise in pairs.
Players stand in the positions as shown on the diagram.

SEQUENCE
**A** hits short serve and steps towards the net with racket held up.
**B** allows shuttle to drop to the floor.
**B** returns the shuttle to **A**.
**A** serves again and repeats the movement.
**A** has five serves and **B** has five serves.

FIG. 141
*6 players*
The players stand in the positions shown in the diagram.

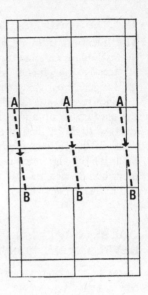

SEQUENCE

**A** serves short and steps forward with his racket head held up.

**B** stands in the receiving position. As **A** serves **B** springs forward towards the net. He meets the shuttle as it crosses the net and dabs it past **A**.

The players change over after five repetitions.

FIG. 142
*9 players*
The players stand in the positions as shown in the
diagram.

A to serve.
B to receive.
C to return a shot from B.

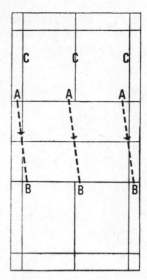

SEQUENCE

A serves short and steps forward with racket held up.

B attacks the serve and hits the shuttle down past A.

C moves and as the shuttle passes A, C hits an underarm clear.

After five repetitions the players move round until each player has a turn in each position.

STAGE 4: SHORT SERVE; RETURN OF SERVE;
UNDERARM CLEAR; SMASH; ATTACK AND
DEFENCE POSITIONS

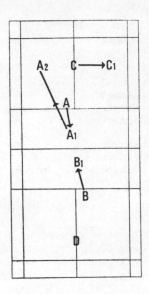

FIG. 143
The players stand on court in positions as shown.

SEQUENCE

**A** serves short and moves in towards the net.

**B** attacks the serve and hits the shuttle past **A**.

**C** plays an underarm clear to the centre of the opposite rear court.

**D** smashes the shuttle straight to the opposite centre and the shuttle is allowed to hit the floor.

*Comment:* When **C** hits an underarm clear, he places his side on the defence. **A** immediately moves away from the net (see diagram) to one side of the court. **C** occupies the other side, level with **A**. Both players face inwards, defending against the straight smash.

As **D** moves to perform the overhead smash, **B** remains at the net. **B** and **D** are in attacking positions (front and back). **C** and **A** are in defensive positions (sides).

After 5 repetitions the players move round one place.

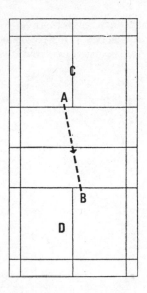

FIG. 144
The players stand in the positions as shown in the
diagram.

SEQUENCE

A serves short and moves forward with his racket held up.

B attacks the serve and hits the shuttle down past A.

C plays an underarm clear.

D moves to attack the shuttle.

A moves back as C moves to the side.

A and C are level with each other in a side formation (see Stage 4).

D plays an overhead clear instead of the smash. He hits the shuttle in the direction of A. This has placed B and D on the defence.

A moves back to hit the shuttle as C moves forwards to the net.

A and C are in an attacking position, i.e. front and back formation.

B moves away from the net to the half court area when he sees that D has hit the shuttle high.

D moves forward to the half court area after his shot.

B and D take up a defensive position. Sides formation.

A plays an overhead smash straight to the centre and the shuttle is allowed to hit the ground.

The game is now open for further development.

After five repetitions of this sequence, move the players round one place. Do this until each player has a turn in each position.

199

STAGE 6: SHORT SERVE; RETURN OF SERVE;
UNDERARM CLEAR; OVERHEAD DROP SHOT;
UNDERARM CLEAR; OVERHEAD SMASH

FIG. 145
The players stand on court in the positions as shown.

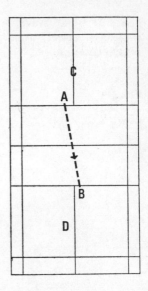

SEQUENCE

A serves short and moves forward with racket head held up.

B attacks the serve, hits the shuttle past A and stays at the net.

C plays an underarm clear and moves to the half court as A retreats to the half court to stand level with C.

D hits the shuttle and plays an overhead drop shot to A.

A moves forward and plays an underarm clear and then returns to his position in the half court area.

D hits the shuttle straight back with an overhead smash. The shuttle is allowed to hit the ground.

After five repetitions of the sequence, the players move round one place.

STAGE 7: SHORT SERVE; RETURN OF SERVE;
UNDERARM CLEAR; OVERHEAD DROP SHOT;
UNDERARM LOW RETURN; UNDERARM CLEAR;
OVERHEAD SMASH

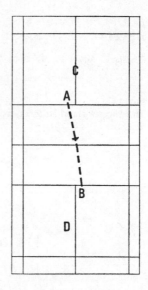

FIG. 146
The players stand on court in the positions as shown
in the diagram.

SEQUENCE

A serves short and moves forwards with his racket head held up.

B attacks the serve, hits the shuttle past A and stays at the net.

C plays an underarm clear and moves to take a position on one side of
the court as A moves away from the net to the half court area.

D hits an overhead drop shot to A.

A steps forward and plays an underarm low return to B.

B plays an underarm clear and then moves back to take up a defensive
position side by side with D.

A stays at the net as C moves back and plays an overhead smash straight
back into the opposite court. The shuttle is allowed to hit the ground.

SUMMARY

The players work through these practices, based on development from a
short serve. The coach should realise that there are other possibilities.
However, by practising the most obvious possibilities the players grasp the
basic principle of attack and defence, and the movements involved during a
realistic situation.

N.B. It will be noted that the server's partner always returns the shuttle
high. This particular shot is used to develop the normal attacking and
defensive positions. The coach should realise that the players should also
try to play low returns whenever possible, in the normal game situation.

201

# DOUBLES TACTICS
# DEVELOPMENT BASED ON A HIGH SERVE

STAGE 1: HIGH SERVE AND OVERHEAD SMASH

FIG. 147
The players stand in the poistions as shown in the diagram.

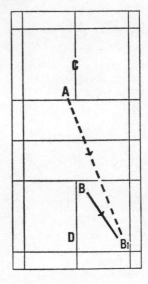

SEQUENCE

A serves high to the forehand corner of B.

A moves back to defend his half of the court.

C moves across to defend his half of the court.

B moves back to play an overhead smash.

D moves into the net.

B and D are in an attacking formation (front and back).

A and C are in a defensive formation (sides).

B hits a straight smash down the line on the backhand side of C.

A and C both turn to the left side of their court.

C defends the smash down the line.

A defends the smash to the centre.

After five repetitions of the sequence the players move round one place.

STAGE 2: HIGH SERVE AND OVERHEAD SMASH

FIG. 148
The players stand in the positions as shown.

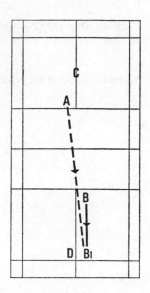

SEQUENCE

A serves high to the centre court (the backhand side of **B**).

**B** moves back to play an overhead smash.

**D** moves quickly in towards the net.

**A** steps back to the half court and faces inwards to defend against the straight smash to the centre.

**C** moves to the side, level with **A** and faces inwards to defend against the straight smash to the centre.

**B** plays an overhead smash and the shuttle is allowed to hit the ground between **A** and **C**.

After five repetitions of the sequence, the players move round one place.

FIG. 149
The players stand in the positions as shown.

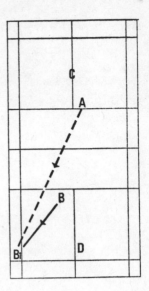

SEQUENCE

A serves high to the backhand corner of B.

B moves back to play an overhead forehand smash.

D moves quickly in towards the net.

C moves to the side and faces outwards to defend against the straight smash down the side line.

A moves back level with C and faces inwards to defend against the smash to the centre.

B smashes the shuttle and it is allowed to hit the ground.

A and C are in the 'sides' defensive formation.

B and D are in the 'front and back' attacking formation.

After five repetitions of the sequence the players move round one place.

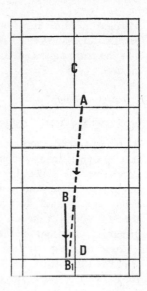

FIG. 150
The players stand in the positions as shown.

SEQUENCE

A serves high to the centre line of B.

B moves back to play an overhead smash straight to the centre.

D moves forward into the net.

A drops back to the half court area to defend against the smash to the centre.

C moves to the side, level with A, and faces inwards to defend against the smash to the centre.

A and C are in the 'sides' defensive formation.

B and D are in the 'sides' attacking formation.

After five repetitions of the sequence, the players move round one place.

*Comments:* If the players occupy the correct positions for each high serve, the coach should have no problem in developing his teaching of Doubles tactics.

There are other possible replies to the high serve, i.e. the drop shot and the overhead attacking clear. However, these are variations for experienced players. The learner should at all times play an overhead smash to the high serve. When he can do this with competence, then is the time to begin varying his possible returns to the high serve.

It is up to the individual coach to decide which strokes take priority over others in any particular situation. The above progressions are an approach to a development of play based on the high serve. The idea is simply to teach the players by creating progressive practices. The coach should establish the

O                    205

situation and then insist upon repetition of that situation until the players become familiar with it. When the players' automatic reaction is to move into the correct position in a familiar situation, the coach has succeeded in his task.

## 46. ORGANISING COMPETITIVE BADMINTON

Match play and tournaments provide the opportunity for players to test their progress in a competitive situation. In practice, the emphasis is on improving the skills. In competition, the emphasis is on winning. The majority of players enjoy winning. They concentrate harder and show more determination and effort in their attempts to win. Competition brings out the best efforts from most players. The result of competition is usually a general improvement in the standard of play.

Apart from the effect on the general standard of play, competition creates tensions and frustrations. Competition is the conflict between two opposing forces with a single aim, i.e. to win the game. Tension and friction are inevitable. A player should experience tension and learn to overcome and control the emotions aroused in him by the competitive situation. This is a factor worth considering in his development as a player and a sportsman.

The coach should organise matches against opposing teams, and tournaments in which the player can test his ability and assess his standard of play against others.

Two types of competitive Badminton are considered:

(1) *Match Play* – One team of players against another team of players.

(2) *Tournament Play*

(a) Singles or Doubles or Mixed Doubles Open Tournament organised on a knock-out basis.

(b) Handicap Tournament of Singles, Doubles and Mixed Doubles organised on a knock-out basis.

(c) American Tournament – achieving the best results from a series of games.

The organisation of competitive Badminton is considered under these categories.

### (1) MATCH PLAY

*The Team:* The team usually consists of six players, arranged in three doubles pairs. Each pair play a contest against each pair of the opposing team.

*The Order of Play:* The pairs in each team are numbered as 1st Pair, 2nd Pair, 3rd Pair.

|       | *Team A* | versus | *Team B* |
|-------|----------|--------|----------|
| Pair  | 1        | v      | 1        |
|       | 2        | v      | 2        |
|       | 3        | v      | 3        |
|       |          |        |          |
| Pair  | 1        | v      | 2        |
|       | 2        | v      | 3        |
|       | 3        | v      | 1        |
|       |          |        |          |
| Pair  | 1        | v      | 3        |
|       | 2        | v      | 1        |
|       | 3        | v      | 2        |

Altogether nine matches are played.

*Organising the Match:* Usually when a match takes place it is between the home team and a visiting team. The visitors are guests of the home team and certain courtesies should be extended to the visiting team.

(1) When arranging the match, also enclose a diagram showing the directions to the venue. There is nothing more frustrating than searching for a building in a maze of streets.

(2) When the visitors arrive, a member of the home team should welcome them and show them to the changing rooms.

(3) Allow the visitors to knock up on court before the match begins. Make a point of doing this so that they can get used to the lighting and the conditions of the court.

(4) Explain which part of the ceiling is considered as a let and which part is a fault.

(5) Provide refreshments during the match and make sure that the visitors are served first.

(6) At the end of the match, the captain of the home team should thank the visitors for the contest.

These are a few courtesies, but essential for developing good social relationships between players.

*Equipment:* For a normal contest of nine matches, two cartons of shuttlecocks should be provided. In match play feathered shuttlecocks are used unless both teams agree to use plastic shuttlecocks.

A scorebook is used to keep a record of games played and points scored. They can be obtained from most sports shops.

(2) TOURNAMENT PLAY

An Open Tournament consisting of Singles, Doubles and Mixed Doubles events.

It is not essential to hold all these events and the number of events will depend on the number of entries for the tournament, or the number of events offered to the players. However, the principle involved for organising an Open Tournament is the same for one event or for five events.

In this tournament all the players start level. The tournament is organised on a knock-out basis. This involves a gradual process of elimination, until two players are left to contest the final.

If the tournament is restricted to the members of one particular club, the players may enter by signing their names on a notice, designating which event they wish to enter.

If the tournament is open to a wider field, entry forms are sent out to surrounding clubs. The entry form should provide the following information:

(1) The name of the tournament.
(2) The venue and directions.
(3) The date of the tournament.
(4) The closing date for entries.
(5) The name and address of the secretary who will receive the entry forms.
(6) The list of events.
(7) The cost of entry for each event.
(8) Any rules and conditions under which the tournament is played.

Once these details have been arranged, and the entries received, the players' names are mixed together and the draw is made.

There may be problems if the number of entries does not permit an even draw. The ideal number of entries which lead to the final two contestants is from 2, 4, 8, 16, 32, 64, etc. If the number of entries is between any of these numbers, several players will begin in either the second or the first round of the tournament. This is arranged to allow the final to be between two players. If this is difficult to arrange, further information may be gained from the *Handbook of the Badminton Association of England.*

## THE TOURNAMENT

### REQUIREMENTS

*Shuttlecocks.* Assess how many matches will be played in the tournament. To be on the safe side, order enough shuttles to allow two for each match.

### RECORDING RESULTS

*Results Sheet:* This should be displayed. It should show the order of the draw and a record of results of matches played.

*Results Slips:* This is a small book containing results slips. A result slip is given to the players for each match. The contents should show the name of the players involved in the match, the event and the court number. At the end of the match, the players should sign and record the result on the result slip before handing it in to the Recorder.

208

*Referee:* The person in charge of the Tournament. He is there to decide on all matters involving disputes and questions concerning the rules. He should keep a copy of the Laws of Badminton available for reference.

*Recorder:* The Recorder keeps a record of the matches to be played and arranges the order of play. He is responsible for keeping the Results Sheet up-to-date as matches are completed.

*Umpire:* The Umpire controls the game and keeps the score for the players. At this level of play, the players should act as Umpires for matches themselves. It is one way in which players can accept additional responsibility and acquire a knowledge of the Laws.

For a small tournament, this type of organisation should be sufficient. Senior Championships will obviously require more officials and a more detailed organisation.

### HANDICAP TOURNAMENTS

A Handicap Tournament is organised in exactly the same way as above. The difference is that the players do not start level. Each player is handicapped according to his ability. The advantage of handicapping is that it gives the weaker player an equal chance of winning against the strong player.

*Example:*

Player **A** is a strong player.

Player **B** is a weaker player.

Player **A** may receive a handicap of minus 10 points. If the game is played up to 15 points, player **A** must score 25 points to win a game.

Player **B** may receive a handicap of plus 5 points. Player **B** only has to score 10 points to win the game.

The game begins at Player **A** minus 10, Player **B** plus 5.

It is important that the varying ability of the players is considered very carefully when giving handicaps.

Handicap tournaments are useful at the beginner level and club level, as the strong player is forced to work hard to score his points and cannot make many mistakes. The weaker player has a chance to go for his shots and can afford to make mistakes and still win. Both players are motivated to play well and the result is usually a general improvement in each player's standard of play.

### AMERICAN TOURNAMENT

In this type of tournament, the players are placed in sections. A player must achieve the most wins in his section to reach the final. This type of tournament can include all the possible events in the game, i.e. Singles, Doubles and Mixed Doubles.

The number of sections arranged are dependent on the number of players. If there are 16 players in a Singles Tournament, there may be four sections. In each section there will be four players. The players in each section will play against each other. The player with the best results wins his section. With four sections, there will be four winners. The winners play off a Semi-Final, and then there is a Final between the winners of the Semi-Finals.

The advantage of this system is that the competitors play more matches and have an increased chance of reaching the Final. In a knock-out tournament, one defeat and the tournament is over for that particular player. In the American tournament, even if a player loses one match, he is still in the tournament and has another chance at winning.

The organisation for the Handicap and American Tournaments is the same as for the Open Tournament. The coach should be aware of the advantages and disadvantages of each system and should be able to organise competitive badminton. These systems are basic ones and the organisation is simple and practical.

## 47. GENERAL INFORMATION

This book has been written for people interested in Badminton, i.e. beginners, players and coaches. Reading a book is sufficient up to a point, but beyond that point is the question of 'How can these different categories be achieved?'

The following information should answer this question.

THE SPORTS COUNCIL

This organisation is a body designed to develop sport in this country. With particular reference to Badminton, the Sports Council in co-operation with Badminton Association of England, organises courses in Badminton. These courses may take the form of a weekend course or a week's course at an established Centre managed by the Sports Council.

These courses include:

(a) a course for beginners

(b) a course for players.

These courses are organised by the Sports Council and the instruction is given by coaches holding a coaching award of the Badminton Association of England.

(c) Courses for players who wish to become coaches.

(d) Courses for coaches who wish to reach a higher coaching grade.

Once again, instruction is given by coaches who hold the coaching awards of the Badminton Association of England.

These different courses take place throughout the country. The Sports

Council will, if requested, send the necessary information and application forms for any particular course. The address to write to is:

The Sports Council,
70 Brompton Road,
London SW3 1EX.

As well as working in co-operation with the Sports Council the Badminton Association of England holds its own coaching courses. These courses have been a feature of the work of the Badminton Association of England during the past ten years. Different courses for coaches of various grades are held throughout England. Any teacher or player wishing to become a coach should write to:

The Coaching Secretary,
B. A. of E.,
44–45 Palace Road,
Bromley,
Kent.

THE BADMINTON ASSOCIATION OF ENGLAND

The Association is governed by a Council of elected representatives of all the County Associations. The majority of Badminton clubs in the country are affiliated to the Badminton Association of England.

If you wish to join a Club in your area and do not know where there is an affiliated club, it is possible to discover one in the following way. Write to the Secretary of the Badminton Association of England. His name and address is:

The Secretary,
44–45 Palace Road,
Bromley,
Kent.

The information you require is the name of the Secretary of your County Association. From the Secretary of your County Association you can obtain a list of the names and addresses of the Secretaries of the affiliated Badminton clubs in your area. Once you have this information, it is an easy step to visit a club and apply for membership.

LOCAL EDUCATION AUTHORITIES

In many towns and cities in the British Isles, the local Education Authority now provides recreational activities in Adult Institutes of Further Education. Badminton is one of these recreational activities. The local education authority is also responsible for the management of Youth Centres, of which many now provide Badminton as a recreational activity. The instructors at these establishments for adults or at the Youth Centres are usually qualified

211

Badminton coaches. The fee required to attend a class is quite small. These centres also provide the necessary equipment, i.e. rackets and shuttlecocks. Many players have learned the game by attending one of these centres. Information about Adult Institutes and Youth Centres can be obtained by writing to your local Education Authority.

SUGGESTIONS FOR READING

The following publications are useful for further information on the game.
(1) *Notes for Badminton Coaches*
    from the Coaching Secretary (see address above).
(2) *The B. A. of E. Handbook*
(3) *The International Badminton Federation Handbook*
(4) *The Badminton Gazette* (the official publication of the B. A. of E.)
These publications can be obtained from:
                    The Secretary,
                        Badminton Association of England,
                            44-45 Palace Road,
                            Bromley,
                            Kent.

PART FOUR

# Competition Badminton

## 48. INTRODUCTION TO PART FOUR

Badminton is a competitive game. Players compete against each other whenever they go onto the court to play a game. Very often in a friendly game the result is of secondary importance to the satisfaction to be gained from a good game. There is usually nothing at stake apart from the enjoyment of playing.

The title *Competition Badminton* draws attention to organised competition, where there is something at stake. An individual player or team of players competes against other individuals or teams for a specific objective i.e., a trophy. Competition ranges from club league matches to Uber Cup and Thomas Cup matches; from club tournaments to the All England Championships. In any form of organised competition, players compete to decide which player or team is the best in that competition. Winning is of primary importance for it is the measure of success in the tournament. This is not to say that enjoyment does not matter for would one play badminton and enter organised competition if one did not enjoy doing so? Does not the enjoyment come from the challenge of competition; to test one's skill against another opponent in the effort to become the best player in the competition?

If winning is of primary importance in competition then the performance the player gives in the game is the determining factor in winning.

A player must enter competitions to improve. The competition is the arena in which one player tests his skill against others. His success or lack of it against different opponents is a measure of his improvement as a player. Each time a player competes the key question is whether or not he can perform successfully against his opponent.

This section is all about performance in competition. It is written with two objectives:

(1) To explain and clarify what is involved in improving performance in in competition.

(2) To provide some practical guidelines on how to improve the performance of a player.

In these respects the club player is no different from the international player. The level at which one plays is only a matter of degree. For this reason the section will be of benefit to all players who enjoy the challenge of organised competition.

215

## 49. PERFORMANCE

The word performance is used in two ways. We distinguish between a successful or unsuccessful performance and a good or poor performance. There is no contradiction to say, 'X lost but he gave a good performance', or 'X won but he played badly'. Successful performance indicates that the player attained his objective; he won the game. To describe a performance as good or poor implies a value judgement about some standard which the player attained or failed to attain. The criteria for evaluating a performance may include reference to the player's skill, i.e., his strokes or tactical ability; to his fitness, i.e., his speed, agility, strength; or to his attitude, i.e., his determination, concentration, commitment etc.

When the word good is used about a performance it should be made clear which aspects of the performance is being judged. This point is of particular importance for coaches. A player may come off the court having lost and one hears the comment 'Well played, better luck next time'. What does 'well played' mean? Unless it is made explicit the statement provides no information and the player learns nothing.

To try to win is what the game is all about. Hence successful performance is the main target. Nevertheless the ideal is to strive to produce both a successful and a good performance. The player should try to win and also try to attain the necessary standards of excellence required in the game. The chances of being successful are increased if the player can also ensure a good performance.

A good performance is one in which the player performs to the best of his ability at the time. Let us concentrate on this aspect of the game.

Performance consists of three main factors:- Skill, Fitness, and Attitude. The chart on page 221 illustrates a simple analysis of these factors.

(A) SKILL

Skill can be divided into (a) Skills of the game, and (b) Games skill.

(a) *Skills of the game.* These are the various hitting techniques and the movement around the court. The emphasis is on playing strokes. Once a stroke has been learnt, it is perfected by constant practice and application in games situations. The standards in stroke production are accuracy, control and economy of effort. The standards in movement are lightness, balance and control. These standards should be the objective each time the player practises. Players often fail to realise this. It is often the case that one can watch players in action and know that they are only practising. It might be because their movements are different to those which they normally perform in a game or because the practice appears to be taken less seriously than a game. For example in practice most players when asked to perform an overhead drop shot do so very obviously. In a game situation it is difficult to distinguish the preparation

216

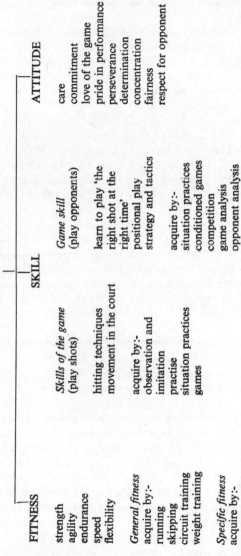

**PERFORMANCE**

**FITNESS**

strength
agility
endurance
speed
flexibility

*General fitness*
acquire by:-
running
skipping
circuit training
weight training

*Specific fitness*
acquire by:-
pressure training
stroke training
shadow badminton
conditioned games

A balanced programme
of Exercise and Rest
and Correct Diet

**SKILL**

*Skills of the game*
(play shots)

hitting techniques
movement in the court

acquire by:-
observation and
imitation
practise
situation practices
games

*Game skill*
(play opponents)

learn to play 'the
right shot at the
right time'
positional play
strategy and tactics

acquire by:-
situation practices
conditioned games
competition
game analysis
opponent analysis

**ATTITUDE**

care
commitment
love of the game
pride in performance
perseverance
determination
concentration
fairness
respect for opponent

for an overhead drop shot from a smash or a clear. This does not make sense. It means that the wrong movements are practised. In practice the player must think about how he is doing what he is doing. A practice session should be taken as seriously as a game. Quality performance is the standard in both practice and competition. Coaches in particular should indicate the standard and ensure that the player works hard to attain it.

(b) *Games skill.* The emphasis is on playing opponents. The player applies his skills to achieve his objective, which is to defeat his opponent and win the game. Games skill is concerned with playing the right shot at the right time and involves tactical play. Therefore the player must learn the basic defensive and attacking positions. He then puts this into practice in conditioned games, and in competition.

In a game a player has to analyse the situations for what they are, make appropriate judgements and a decision to play a particular shot. To do this involves both a critical understanding of the games situations and a knowledge of one's opponent. A player can only acquire such knowledge by asking the relevent questions. The two methods of analysis which follow illustrate the sorts of questions one might ask and the sort of knowledge one will gain.

SITUATION ANALYSIS This method is used to assist a player to analyse an opponent's game and to make the right shot at the right time. What is involved in playing the right shot at the right time? To do so requires judgement of the situation and the decision to play the appropriate shot. For example a player may be deep in the forehand corner and his opponent waiting ready in the centre. What is the best shot to play in this situation? Is it a clear, a drive down the line, or a cross-court sliced drop shot? How does one decide which shot to play? This requires a judgement of the situation and a quick decision before acting. It may take only a fraction of a second to judge the situation and make the decision. All this requires knowledge. A knowledge which may be gained from years of experience of similar situations but nevertheless is relevant knowledge. It is knowledge of oneself, the behaviour of the shuttle, and the opponent.

Before a player knows which type of shot to play in a situation he should first decide what sort of situation he is in. If we return to our example, we realise that the player would hardly play a flat cross-court smash from deep in the forehand corner with the opponent waiting ready in the centre. The reasons are obvious, and there are reasons. There are reasons why he might play a clear, for it would be a safe shot in the situation. There are also reasons why he might play a smash down the line, or a sliced cross-court drop shot. These are rather more complicated but nevertheless possible factors for dicussion. In this example we might all agree that the player is in a position where he cannot do much with the shuttle. On the other hand he might be standing in the centre with the shuttle floating just above the net. Obviously to clear in this situation would be ridiculous. One might drop shot but most effective would be to smash it to the ground. There are several possibilities though we might all agree that the player is in a situation where he can do something with the shuttle.

*Basic Situation:* It is possible to establish two basic situations in the game of badminton.

(1) Situations where one cannot do much with the shuttle.

(2) Situations where one can do something with the shuttle.

Numerous examples could be given of various situations in the court but all can be narrowed down to these two. Both players and spectators can recognise when a player is in one of these two situations. If this is the case in a game then a player must at one time or another be in one of these two situations. His problem is to decide what to do in the situation. There are obviously numerous types of shots he could play and it is not possible to cover all the different positions he may find himself in on the court. Luckily all the different replies can be simplified. A player in any of the basic situations can follow several rules which govern his decision to play a particular shot.

(1) He can give his opponent a shot he cannot do much with (safe shot).

(2) He can do something with it (try for the winner).

(3) He can try to force his opponent to give him a shot he can do something with.

(4) He can give his opponent a shot which he can do something with.

(5) He can do nothing with it (make an error).

These are the five basic possibilities from each of the two basic situations.

It might be clearer to examine this in the following chart.

Examine the first situation in the chart, (shots you cannot do much with) and look along the column of possible replies. Some idea of the sort of things you should or should not do in the situation begin to emerge.

In the first situation if you cannot do much at all at least you could do the first one and give your opponent a shot he cannot do much with. In the next column it would be a bit rash to do something with it, (go for the winner). No. 3 would be positive badminton; No. 4 ridiculous; and No. 5 unforgivable.

Now examine the second basic situation (where you can do something with the shuttle) and examine the column of possible replies. No. 1 would be alright but rather negative badminton and almost a chance missed. No. 2 would be positive attacking badminton and appropriate to go for the winner. No. 3. would be a sound tactic to force a weak return and set it up for the outright winner. No. 4 would be unforgivable; and No. 5 would be sheer stupidity (though to err is human).

This simple analysis covers all the possible situations which might occur in the game of badminton and prescribes the possible action in any situation.

| | 1 | 2 | 3 | 4 | 5 |
|---|---|---|---|---|---|
| | Give opponent a shot he cannot do much with | Do something with it. (Try for winner) | Force opponent to give you a shot you can do something with | Give opponent a shot he can do something with | Do nothing with it. |
| Situation 1 Cannot do much with the shuttle | | | | | |
| Situation 2 Can do something with the shuttle | | | | | |

220

There are obviously many types of shots but all must meet these conditions. Obviously if one considers a game and thinks of two fit and talented players who give each other shots they cannot do much with, the game could last indefinitely. Perhaps each in turn would send the occasional weak return or make an error but things being equal this would even out and the result would be stalemate. The attacking type of player accepts the situation where he cannot do much with the shuttle and gives the same sort of reply. However he constantly strives to force the sort of return from his opponent which puts him in a position where he can do something with the shuttle.

The question is 'How do you get your opponent to give you a situation where you can do something with the shuttle?' Here are a few possible answers.

(1) Outmanoevre him. Hit to the spaces and move him away from his centre until he is slow to recover and leaves a gap.

(2) Tire him. Prolong the rallies until he tires and cannot cover the court. Fitness is essential here.

(3) Upset his game.

   (a) change the speed.

   (b) change directions.

   (c) alter the rhythm. i.e. slow the game down or speed it up.

   (d) use variations—different types of shot and speeds.

(4) Deceive him. Disguise your intentions.

   (a) Pretend to do one thing and then do another.

   (b) delay your shot and make him commit himself to a movement before you hit the shuttle.

   (c) eliminate stroke habits. Make your preparation look identical for similar shots then your opponent will not know where the shuttle is going until you actually hit it.

(5) Play to his weaknesses. You do this so that you can predict the return or know he is likely to make a weak return or an error.

(6) Play to his strengths. It is sometimes necessary to do this because you can predict what he is likely to do with the shuttle. If everything else has been tried it might be the last resort. You might for example give your opponent an easy shot on his forehand knowing he will attempt a straight smash. You can anticipate this shot and try to cut it off and play it to the open court and perhaps force him in return to give you a shot you can do something with.

This analysis provides quite sound guidelines to determine what sort of things you should do in a situation. When someone offers advice, such as you should do this or that shot it is a simple matter to understand why. Whatever advice is given must be based on reasons which satisfy these simple principles.

This is the special knowledge required by a player. It can be learnt and understood by beginners. The beginner will obviously need more time to realise what sort of situation he is in. He will consider all the factors and his judgement of the situation may be wrong; so he makes the wrong decision and plays the wrong shot. He is also limited by his fitness or ability. He might assess the situation correctly, i.e. he might be at the centre and the shuttle about shoulder height on his backhand side, in a situation where he can do something with it. However he cannot take advantage of the situation because he cannot play backhand shots.

The experienced player has the advantage because he has experienced more numerous situations and in the time has learnt more strokes. He has learnt what to do in the situation by trial and error. He appears to play by instinct and yet really plays by recognising the situation for what it is, makes a rapid decision and an appropriate shot. It might be a sound idea to examine a few basic types of player and apply this analysis to them.

*The Retriever:* Whatever situation this type of player is in he can be relied upon to get it back and keep it in play. He might be in a position where he cannot do much with the shuttle or where he can do something with it. In either situation he simply returns the shuttle to place his opponent in a position where he cannot do much with the shuttle. His badminton is negative. You can rely on him never to attempt the winner, which when you consider it is a useful bit of information.

*The Gambler:* Whatever situation this player is in he attempts to hit winners. Someone has most probably told him to attack all the time and this he tries to do. For he fails to make the distinction between an attacking attitude and attacking strokes. He has failed to realise that there are situations where you cannot do much with the shuttle in which case it is better to place your opponent in the same sort of situation, or try to force your opponent to give you a situation where you can do something with the shuttle.

The players in both of these examples though extreme types are typical of many young players. They fail to recognise a situation for what it is and let their passions and not their judgement rule their decision to play a particular shot.

It is possible to apply this analysis to any player. Young players are often told to learn by watching top class players in action. They are told to study their opponents game. It is surprising how many do this but have not the faintest idea of what sort of things to look at. They often return with snippets of information about strokes or things which impressed them. Things like, 'a good backhand' or 'a strong smash', 'very fast about the court', or 'loses his temper easily'. This is useful information if considered in the context of the situation it was played in but absolutely useless as an observation in isolation.

Players should use this analysis and look carefully at what a top class player does in a situation. One might go further than this and suggest that whatever level of play you participate in, whether it is club play or International play observe the top players in your area. What sort of things do they do in a situation where they can do something with the shuttle? What sort of things do they do in a situation where they cannot do something with the shuttle? Look at play from this point of view and you will gain insight into your own game and that of other players.

Though experience is a vital factor in the development of the player it is not the sole factor determining the amount of knowledge a player can gain about the game. From the beginning any player can learn to recognise these situations and to use his judgement based on sound reasons in deciding what sort of shot to play.

PLAYER ANALYSIS

This system is used to gain more information about an opponent. It is simply a questionnaire which focuses attention on particular aspects of an opponent's game. A player who completes questionnaires on other players can build up a file which can be referred to whenever necessary. At the same time it assists a player to learn to analyse an opponent's game. Assume one is due to play a strong opponent. A study of the questionnaire will indicate that opponent's favourite shots; his movement patterns; his replies to a particular order of shots. It is possible to be prepared with a good insight into the opponent's game and to have already worked out the opponent's possible replies in certain situations. With practice one can build up a complete picture of the opponent's game.

## Questionnaire

1. Name of Player
2. Age
3. Ranking
4. Physical build—tall, medium, small/heavy, light, muscular/gymnastic, athletic.
5. Results this season (only good opponents)
    Won—name opponent
    Lost—name opponent

### Things to look for

1. SERVE
    (a) Does he/she serve high, i.e. very high or medium arc.
    (b) When does he/she serve low (from forehand or backhand of court)
    (c) Any points about receiving serve.
        Where does he/she position herself?
        Does he smash short serve?
        What does he do with short serve?
        Does he ever drop off high serve and when?
    (d) Where is the serve placed. Centre or side.

223

## 2. CENTRAL BASE
During rally—does he/she have a forward base?
—does he/she have a backward base?

## 3. STROKES
### OVERHEAD STROKES
*Clears*    (a) When he clears from backhand side—is it backhand or round head
        (b) When does he clear most?
        (c) Where does he clear to?

*Drops*    (a) What situation does he drop from?
        (b) What sort of drop shot, sliced, etc?
        (c) Where to?

*Smash*    (a) When does he smash? i.e. from forehand, backhand, $\frac{1}{2}$-court, etc.
        (b) Where to? i.e. straight across court.
        (c) What type? i.e. half, full, slice, steep, etc.

### UNDERARM STROKES
*Receiving* (a) Which side does he defend on mainly?
*smash*    (b) Does he return smash with drop or clear?
        (c) Any favourite direction, i.e. across court or straight?
        (d) Any difference forehand or backhand side?

*Receiving* What does he do with drop shot?
*drop*    (a) return drop
        (b) clear
        (c) hold and flick

*Back of* What does he do if caught at the back in a low position
*Court*    (a) on forehand side—clear or drop?
        (b) on backhand side—clear or drop—Where?

## 4. DECEPTION
Does he use it?
Any particular shot, or situation?
If so what does he do?

## 5. FAVOURITE STROKE

## 6. WEAKEST STROKE

## 7. STRATEGY—TACTICS
(a) What sort of situation does he appear to like best?
(b) Does he have any particular tactic which you have noticed?

## 8. FITNESS
(a) Speed about court.
(b) Does he play full out all the time?
(c) Does he get out of breath easily?
(d) What is he like after a long hard rally—
    (i)   if he wins it?
    (ii)  if he loses it?
(e) After such a rally does he appear to recover quickly—
    (i)   be able to play another long rally?
    (ii)  begin to rush his shots and try for quick winners?
    (iii) make mistakes?

(f) Does fatigue affect his movements, if so how?
    (i) speed or reaction?
    (ii) travelling backwards?
    (iii) recovering to centre?
    (iv) travelling forwards—does he take shuttles high at net?
                        —does he take shuttles low?

9. GENERAL
What sort of player is he—
(a) Likes long rallies?
(b) Defensive—tends to wait for mistake?
(c) Attacking—goes for winners, etc?
(d) Plays a fast game?
(e) Plays a slow game?
(f) Confident?
(g) What is he like in a tense situation—
    (i) cool?
    (ii) nervous?
(h) Anything else you can think of?

(B) FITNESS

The chart on page 217 illustrates the main components in fitness and the methods used to attain fitness. Section 2 (Training for Badminton) explains fitness in detail.

As a player improves in his performance and moves into higher levels of play so the need for fitness becomes more important. Equal consideration must be given to exercise, rest and correct diet. Specific fitness training is a highly specialised business and to train properly it is recommended that expert advice is obtained before a programme is devised. A player should make certain he is in good health and medically able to withstand the rigours of training. A visit to the doctor for a check up is well advised. Correct diet is also essential and once again advice from a doctor or a dietician is necessary.

The actual balance between exercise, rest and diet is one which the player must discover for himself. It is often a matter of feeling right and no one but the player can decide that.

(C) ATTITUDE

The third major factor in performance is attitude. It is a difficult subject to write about. Usually discussion about attitude is to be found in the study of psychology, and philosophy. The area is very complex. However as it is such an important factor in the development of players and essential to perform-ance, some discussion about attitude must be included. In the chart (page 221) I have written a list of words descriptive of what I consider to be an appro-priate attitude to the game. The following discussion will make clear why these particular characteristics are selected.

There has been much written about the means of acquiring skill and fitness (see sections 1 and 2). The fact that both are essential to performance

225

is shown by the range of strokes and the athletic ability many players now possess. Gone are the days when players just knocked up and played games. Now there are a great variety of means to skill and fitness involving work on and off the court. Added to this is the detail paid to footwear and clothing for ease of movement and the design of rackets to facilitate racket head control and increase hitting power.

With all this behind him it is only natural for the player to expect to perform well. He may win or lose without detracting from his good performance which is usually assessed by the sort of remark, 'I played well'. Alternatively he may leave the court dissatisfied with his performance and return to work at that factor which he believed was responsible. Often this is to do with skill or fitness and the remedy is usually some intense physical work e.g. practice or training.

Not to be forgotten is the player who complains about 'tensing up' and how doing so caused him to pull away from shots or to hit wildly and make mistakes. The player who complains of feeling 'weak in the legs' and finds it difficult to run during the game, or who excuses himself on the grounds of, 'I couldn't seem to keep my mind on the game.' 'I couldn't be bothered,' or 'I felt fed up.' All these examples have in common the fact that they are connected with the player's feeling and emotions. Emotions affect the manner in which he applies himself to the game; what we usually describe as attitude. A player who produces a poor performance because of his thoughts and feelings may be said to have an inappropriate attitude to the game. Attitude is inextricably bound up with skill and fitness in contributing to good performance. All three factors are interrelated, any one can affect the others. Skill will disappear as fatigue appears. Weakness in technique, e.g. serve breaking down, may result in a loss of confidence and a reduced effort. There are numerous examples familiar to all players. Physical work is necessary to improve skill and fitness. The problem arises when the cause of a poor performance is attitude. Feelings and emotions are affected. What is the answer in this situation? One cannot work physically at attitude. Yet just as it is easy to recognise when a poor performance is due to lack of skill or fitness so is it easy to recognise when it is due to an inappropriate attitude. Advice is given which draws attention to the problem. 'You don't seem to care very much,' or 'You don't try hard enough.' The player knows this already but receiving advice is one thing, following it on court is another. There is no easy solution to the problem. The answer involves much discussion and raises many other questions about problems of concern to philosophers and psychologists.

Often players behave on court in ways which are socially frowned upon. They may curse loudly, hit shuttles out of court, throw the racket down, all in sudden outbursts which disappear as quickly as they appear. Sometimes this form of behaviour might be necessary as a release of some emotion, for it benefits the player and helps him to give a good performance. It is important to recognise a distinction between the forms of behaviour which aid and those which hinder performance.

Two aspects will be considered. Firstly, that behaviour which is symptomatic of an inappropriate attitude to the game which results in poor performance. Such discussion will be of benefit to coaches for it will draw attention to some of the problems concerning the coaching of players. Secondly, that behaviour which is symptomatic of an appropriate attitude to the game and which may contribute to a good performance.

One way to get closer to the problem is to ask the question, 'Why does the player behave as he does on the court?' Usually it is in specific situations or phases of the game that behaviour which indicates an inappropriate attitude seems to occur. It is also possible for a player to adopt an inappropriate attitude prior to going on court and as a result give a poor performance. Perhaps the answer lies in how the player assesses what he is doing on the badminton court i.e. how he sees his role, and how he assesses the events that occur during play and their consequences. How does he assess a bad line call, an unforced error, a match against a very strong opponent or an outstanding and highly rated younger player? How does he assess the importance of winning or losing a particular match? These sorts of situations evoke emotional responses which cause players to behave in a way which affects performance.

Take the example of the player expecting to win against an 'inferior' opponent and who, having lost the first set, is 8–10 down in the second set. Suddenly he begins to snatch at the shuttle, plays tentatively and so loses the match. He suffered from 'nerves', seized up, and his skill became affected. One reason perhaps is that at that stage of the game he thought that he might lose. What would the consequences of losing be? To fail to win against such a player, how stupid he would be, what would people think, and how he would appear a failure to his fellow players? He sees the result as having social consequences affecting his status in the eyes of his peers, damaging his self-image. So he experiences the emotion of fear and his behaviour on court is affected accordingly. He tenses up and fails to perform with his usual expertise.

Another example is the player who adopts an inappropriate attitude prior to going on court. He has a fear that he might not perform well and lose the match. Losing would have the same sort of consequences for him as the player in the previous example. This player goes on court already prepared to lose. He doesn't bother to try to win; attempts shots which are not possible; dramatises shots that he misses with appeals to the heavens. He adopts a couldn't care less attitude and may fool around during the match. When he comes off the court having lost, he has already made his excuses on the court. Wasn't it obvious that he hadn't tried and how can one be said to have failed unless one tries first? He has separated losing from failing as a person in this way, for he can always say, 'Ah yes, but if I had really tried I could have won.' Why doesn't he try to win? The answer could be that he doesn't want to harm his self-image so he adopts a tactic to avoid doing that. If he tries he must commit himself fully to the task of winning. This requires an honest attempt to win and his efforts are exposed to the judgement of others. Believing that failure in the game is synonymous with failure as a person, losing is a blow to his self esteem. The consequences of the result are too important to him personally for him to risk an honest performance. In trying to deceive his audience he deceives himself.

These examples though common to many players do draw attention to the fact that a precondition of knowing why a player behaves in different ways is the study of his particular beliefs and values. A person usually responds emotionally in a situation according to how he assesses it. For example the emotion of fear is only experienced when a person appraises a situation as threatening. We usually experience an emotion when we make an appraisal of some kind or other. We experience different emotions when we make different appraisals. In other words emotions are basically forms of cognition.

How a player appraises a situation in the game may be determined by what he sees himself doing on a badminton court. Some idea may be gleaned from answering questions to do with why the person plays badminton. The usual answers to this question are, 'for enjoyment', 'because I like it', 'because I want to play for the County', 'because it makes me feel important', or 'I want to be All England champion'. These are conventional answers, and do not tell one much about the player. Very often there is a conceptual problem. Though these words are used their meaning and implications are not fully appreciated by the player. Any analysis of the reasons also requires clarification of the meaning of the words used. The player plays for enjoyment, but what is enjoyment and what sorts of things in badminton give enjoyment? Questioning and discussion on this level, the constant probing, can clarify much of the muddled thinking that might affect a player's behaviour on court.

A player might say he wants to be the All England champion. This is a worthy ambition for a talented and promising player, but does he know what it implies to be an All England champion? For unless the reasons for this aim are clear and he realises the implications of the task, it will remain a vague ambition. To grasp the concept of being All England champion he must possess some knowledge and understanding of what is required. Once he grasps this he can take steps towards the realisation of this ambition. The practical work required regarding skill and fitness is comparatively easy to work out and a programme may be planned for a player. To realise such an ambition the player must also possess the belief that he is capable of succeeding. Only then will the work become meaningful. His attitude, determined by his beliefs, is again linked with his skill and fitness in contributing towards a good performance.

By careful questioning it is possible to arrive at answers which give apparent reasons for why the player does what he does on the court. These can be classified into those which are relevant to the actual game and those which have no bearing on it. For example, to play because it makes one feel important may be a good reason for taking up the game and persisting at it, but this particular feeling is totally irrelevant in the context of the game and may indeed upset the performance. On the other hand, playing because one enjoys outwitting the opponent in games is going to improve performance, for the thoughts will be involved with the game objectively and one will enjoy the opportunity to test one's skill and not to improve the self-image. There is much confusion in this area and it is not often clear how players do view their participation in a game. It is sometimes very difficult to separate performance in badminton from life in general. The self-image becomes dependent on how a player sees himself in a social context and a sports context and sometimes he finds it difficult to assess his performance seperately in the different contexts.

Knowledge of the player's beliefs and values enables one to discuss the underlying rationale and to assess their validity. For example, do other people think that if you fail to win on court that you are a failure as a person? That if you do a silly shot you are silly? I would suggest that the facts do not support this assumption and it is a false belief. Should a player go on court and expect to win? Has anyone the right to predict the result before the contest begins? Should a friend or a coach say 'You ought to win this one easily'. Does this not show a lack of respect for an opponent who is a person also with a certain competence in the game? Does not this sort of statement also add pressure to the player? He now has extra responsibility for he is expected to do something, to be successful in the match, and what happens during the match if he begins to doubt his ability to win. He may experience fear at the consequences of losing, fear of failure, failure as a person.

I mentioned that players become confused with the self-image in social and sports contexts. Yet how one behaves in a social context is usually determined by the rules and conventions of society and in the different situations one encounters in a society one may adopt a particular role. It might be possible to develop an appropriate attitude to the game and ensure a good performance if players knew what sort of situation they were in and the sort of role they should adopt. Any attempt along these lines would require the logical construction of a model of the game and then a look at the sort of behaviour appropriate to play the game. Such a model might be as follows.

(1) The game is a battle. The battle is between two opponents who present each other with a problem. The problem is how to overcome the opponent and win the battle.

(2) The deciding factor is 'thinking'. You have to think to solve the problem presented by the opponent who not only tries to prevent you winning the battle but also tries to win himself.

(3) You are helped in this battle by the weapons you possess. Your strokes are the weapons but they only hit the shuttle to those places you decide the shuttle shall go.

(4) The decision to hit the shuttle to a particular place is made according to the way you assess what is required to win the battle and is determined by what your opponent does and where he is on the court.

(5) A player with many strokes has many more weapons to use and many more possible solutions to the problem. However these only overcome the problem if used at the right time.

(6) A player with less strokes has less solutions to the problem and so must try to win the battle with what strokes he has. He has a bigger problem. He has to make do with what he has got.

(7) Sometimes strokes do not work as well as usual. A player must accept this fact, adapt his game and try to solve the problem and win the battle with the strokes that do work. A STROKE IS ONLY AS GOOD AS THE RESULT IT ACHIEVES.

(8) With humans mistakes are inevitable in a battle. In this game players have the chance to recover from a mistake and still keep in the battle. Mistakes must be accepted as part of the battle and part of the problem. A player who accepts them will try to correct them while the battle is on.

(9) As a battle is neither won or lost before it has begun, nor is it over until the rules declare one side to be the winner, no player should expect to win or lose a battle before it begins or before it has ended.

(10) Winning is the prize for overcoming the problems presented by the opponent throughout the battle.

(11) Once you enter the battle you must see what you can do to win with what you have got working for you at the time. It is all you can do.

(12) In a badminton battle, victory or defeat is never for all time. The loser always lives to fight another day.

This sort of model equates badminton with a game like chess in which playing is an intellectual exercise and the game becomes a 'battle of wits'. From this model it is possible to work out the sort of attitude appropriate to play the game.

Firstly is there anything about the game itself which gives an indication of the characteristics required to play it? Badminton is an activity that goes on for some time and in which a large degree of skill and judgement is called for. It is the exercise of skill which makes the game so interesting to the players. Just like any other activity which is absorbing, is it absorbing for the interest it holds, which is intrinsic to it. The game is played for its own sake. To play the game well the player has to pay attention to what is going on. To play the game seriously requires discipline. Discipline conveys the idea of submission to rules or some kind of order. This is an important aspect of the game and perhaps requires further explanation.

*Discipline:* What aspects of the game must the player conform to? He must submit himself to the rules of the game, for it is the rules which distinguish badminton from other games. He must conform to the established rules of procedure. However there is an additional factor. The game is also a part of life for a player plays with and against other persons. Interpersonal relationships are involved which presupposes certain conditions governing the behaviour during the game. His interpretation of the rules of the game and conduct within it are determined not only by the rules of the game but also by moral 'rules'. The rules of the game determine what sorts of movements and actions are permissible during the game. The moral 'rules' determine the manner in which one plays the game. To play the game in the 'right spirit' is not simply a request for more enthusiasm but also an appeal that morality shall prevail. Hence respect for the other player, appreciation of his efforts, consideration of his interests, fairness and sportsmanship are all necessary to playing the game. Too often players fail to appreciate the moral aspect of participation in games to the detriment of their performance and to the detriment of the game as an enjoyable activity. To submit to the moral order requires discipline.

Performance also involves skill and fitness. What demands must the player submit to in these areas? The higher the level of performance required the greater are the demands on the player. Badminton is a stern task master. Let me explain.

A player must acquire the skills of the game before he can play the game. To do so requires practice, the repetition of strokes and their application in competition. The advanced game is more complex and requires more concern for perfection. At international level the strokes must be performed with accuracy and control at great speed. To attain this standard of excellence the player must submit himself to practise and perform much rigorous physical work. Fitness is crucial to high skill development. Training on and off the court requires continual discipline. Fitness involves a balance of exercise, rest and diet. The highest standard is the potential maximum fitness of the player. The rigours of training required to reach this standard eliminate anything which is detrimental to this end. Players who do not maintain regular training sessions; who do not work hard in training; who over-eat; or drink too much alcohol; and fail to get their necessary sleep, will find if difficult to attain the standard. Such discipline is imposed by the game for it is intrinsic to the game at that level of play. Once these standards are made clear the responsibility rests with the player. If he wants to attain standards, he must necessarily submit himself to the work required.

As badminton is a voluntarily chosen activity it would seem that the player considers it worthy of his attention. He might be said to have a love for the game for what it has to offer as an opportunity to exercise his skill and judgement. One might therefore expect him to care about how he performs in the game not for what he can get out of it extrinsically, i.e. prestige, money, travel, etc., but purely for the interest it holds. He will care because having chosen the game as worthy of his attention then it matters to his pride that he performs well.

COMPETITION

The game involves competition, for in it the players compete against each other for the object of the game, to win. What are the implications of competition for the players? First, both players must want to win. Second, one player's winning must exclude the other player's winning. Third, both players should persist in trying to win the contest even when they know one of them must fail to win.

Any player who participates in a game is fully committed to try to win and persists in his efforts until the game is ended. A player who does not compete on these terms may be on the court making the recognised movements of the game and yet not playing the game we know as badminton. He is doing something else, playing his own private game, (perhaps where the purpose is to try not to win). We may therefore add determination to persistence as a logical requirement of the game, for what is determination if not seriously trying to win?

It would seem that the characteristics of an appropriate attitude to badminton are implicit in the nature of the game. The fact that two players agree to contest a game implies that they accept certain standards as the logical outcome of that agreement to compete in a game. The implication of the rules and the necessary conditions of competition logically compel players to behave in a certain manner and to try to satisfy specific standards of performance. The enjoyment of the game comes as much from satisfying the standards implicit in the game, in giving a good performance, as in winning. It is probable that the attainment of these standards will bring about a successful performance.

Many players do play the game in such a way as to demonstrate these qualities. The relevant question is that concerned with to what extent they do demonstrate them. When the player begins to improve and progress into higher levels of competition the game becomes very demanding. More time and hard work, and greater personal sacrifice is required to meet the demands. It is at this point that players begin to stop making progress.

One may ask how much care and commitment are involved. How much do players love the game? Now comes the test not of character, but of commitment, of value for the player. The answer involves a realistic appraisal of one's attitude to the game and is of importance for any improvement in the performance.

At this stage it may be of value to sum up so far. I have tried to explain some of the factors involved in the performance of a player. Performance involves skill, fitness and attitude. These three features are interconnected. The words we use are descriptive of an appropriate attitude to the game, and are really intrinsic to the game. Determination, concentration, perseverance, care, commitment, etc, etc., describe how a player should behave if he wants to ensure a good performance. These are the standards which derive from the nature of the activity. It is to these standards the player must submit himself. The degree to which he does so is a measure of his commitment to the game.

Against this background it is now possible to offer some guidance and suggestions on the preparation of players and teams for competitions. The next part is written mainly for the coach but there is no reason why a player cannot use the information to plan his own training programmes.


## 50. PREPARATION FOR AND PARTICIPATION IN COMPETITION

There are a vast number of factors to be considered. The complexity of a detailed discussion is beyond the scope of this book. It is only possible to draw attention to those factors which are essential in the preparation of players for competition.

The preparation of a player or team of players will vary according to the ability and personality of the player, the coach, the time and facilities available and the level of competition. For these reasons it is not possible to be very specific. General principles and considerations will be outlined and whenever possible the details will be added. The emphasis will be on coaching at international level of play. This way attention can be focused on the full range of factors which must be considered in coaching players.

PLANNING A PROGRAMME

(a) *Means/end model.* Consider the whole enterprise and plan a suitable programme. The framework of a plan is relatively simple, e.g. a means/end model. To plan what you intend to do without knowing what your aim is, is like going on a journey without knowing your destination. It does not make sense. The first task is to decide the aim of the whole programme. The aim is usually to defeat a particular player or to win a particular tournament. The measure of improvement in a player's performance is his success in attaining this aim.

233

Now it is possible to consider the particular means required to attain the selected end. What are the requirements of the task? Certain objectives occur according to the aim and the player. Factors such as skill, fitness, knowledge of the game, and attitude would be considered. What sort of things must be learned and practised to develop these factors? Particular forms of training and different skill practices constitute the content of the programme.

To sum up is simple. Select your target (the aim) and decide what sort of work (content) is necessary to attain that target.

(b) *Duration of programme:* The target may be anything from six months to one year ahead. The programme must encompass the whole period. For this reason it is unwise to be too rigid. Players are not machines and coaches do not possess certain knowledge that what they do will work in each individual case. There is no guarantee that the content or the method will be successful. Throughout the whole period the work requires constant evaluation and modification. Allow for a flexible framework for the programme.

(c) *Progression.* There are logical and psychological considerations in any programme. The coach will be wise to reflect on both before commencing. Certain skills presuppose the possession of others. For example one would not expect a player to assume a forward singles base and take the shuttle early if he did not possess the strokes or the speed to do so. Or to smash from the rear court and cut off the return at the net if he did not possess the speed in recovery to do so. It would be unwise to demand standards of excellence at the end of a long match unless the player was fit enough to maintain the pace. To develop fitness is a gradual affair and involves a balance between quantity and quality. Psychological considerations arise in any new development of a player's game. To ask too much from the player in the early stages, to get him to attempt work which he is not capable of, and to expose him to failure and hence frustration at his lack of ability to succeed can result in a loss of confidence in himself and in his coach. This sort of factor is a usual consideration in teaching. If the work is too easy, then boredom arises; if it is too difficult, frustration arises. Such development is a gradual affair of building, and the player will benefit and his confidence will grow if he sees and feels an improvement in skill and fitness.

For these reasons the work may be divided into phases which lead towards the aim of the programme. An example of such a programme could be as follows.

*First phase:*

(1) General fitness training with work on running, skipping, circuit training, and flexibility exercises. An initial preparation for specific work.
(2) Introduction to new hitting techniques or methods of moving on the court. Learn these and practise them.

234

*Second phase:*
(1) Reduce general training and incorporate specific fitness training on the court. The work may include less running and skipping and exercises, added to by stroke practices and sequence work on the court.
(2) The new skills can now be placed into pressure situations and incorporated into games play in the form of conditioned games.
*Third phase:*
(1) Emphasis on specific work. The fitness training will still continue but with the emphasis on quality and not quantity. Stroke practices and sequence work can be completed at a faster rate. Place the emphasis on taking the shuttle much earlier and do the work accordingly on speed of movement.
(2) Greater concentration now on playing games and tournament play.
Throughout the whole period maintain regular checks on the programme. Fitness can be measured regularly against the clock or according to the increase in the quantity of work. The player's weight, and diet require constant observation and due concern should be paid to the general feeling of well being of the player. This is important and the player is the best judge of his condition. If he feels stronger, quicker, and more alert, etc., it is usually a good indication that the programme is well balanced. A player who feels jaded, tired, and discouraged or is generally unhappy with the way he feels is obviously a sign that the programme is not adequate for his individual needs. Each player is a unique individual and it is well to remember this when working on a programme.

(*d*) *Schedules:* It will be obvious that planning a programme is a complex business. It is necessary to keep a record of the work the player does. There are various ways of doing this. There follows now an example of the sort of programme recorded in a form used by the author when coaching international players. The various charts cover all aspects of the work and provide clear directions for the player. One copy of the programme will be given to the player and one copy is kept by the coach. The work is elected from the training methods described in section 2 of this book.
Sheet A provides instructions for the programme.
Sheet B sets out a stroke practice programme for the player.
Sheet C sets out the stroke training programme. This is based on the sequence work and provides the most important section of the programme. It is arranged in the form of a circuit. The page number refers to the page number of the book.
Sheet D is a chart which enables a record to be kept of all the work completed. Each column is headed by a particular aspect of the work. The chart is for a period of four weeks. Each square contains four boxes. Each box represent one week. For example see Monday under 'Exercises'. The first and second boxes contain ticks to indicate that the work has been completed

for weeks 1 and 2. The third box contains a cross to indicate that the player missed his training on that day. The fourth box is empty which indicates that the player has not yet reached that day. If a player misses training for any reason he makes a comment on the appropriate line in the section under comments. In this way the coach can maintain a careful check on the player's progress and make any modifications of the programme as and when necessary.

*Exercises*
Do circuit training schedule. 3 repetitions of circuit.
On the press-ups ensure that you complete the full range of movement in the
arms and shoulders. Go through the three circuits smoothly and rhythmically
without a pause. Repeat daily. Rest one day a week.

*Skipping*
Weeks 1 and 2. Ten minutes daily.
Method. Skip 2 minutes, rest one minute until ten minutes skipping is completed.
Weeks 3 and 4. Fifteen minutes daily.
Method. Skip 3 minutes, rest one minute until fifteen minutes skipping is
         completed.
Rest one day a week.

*Running*
Weeks 1 and 2. Fifteen minutes jogging.
Weeks 3 and 4. Thirty minutes. 15 minutes jogging and then 15 minutes at a
         faster pace.
Try to maintain a good posture and develop a rhythm.
Do this 5 days a week.

*Practice*
Stroke practice programme. 2–3 times a week.
Stroke training programme. 2–3 times a week.
Do on alternate days. Emphasise quality—lightness about the court, accuracy
and control.

*Games*
Play as often as possible. Concentrate on doing the basic things correctly.
Good positioning behind the shuttle and accuracy and control in the shots.

STROKE PRACTICE PROGRAMME

*Name* A. BROWN        *Duration*    4 Weeks    *Dates*

| STROKE | INSTRUCTIONS | REPETITIONS |
|---|---|---|
| *Overhead Clear* | (2 steps into the centre after each shot) | |
| 1. Fh. clear. | Rally between A and B. | 50 |
| 2. Fh. and Bh, clear. | A bh. clear—B fh. clear (down the line) | 20 backhand |
| 3. ,, | Change over. | 20 ,, |
| 4. Fh. and Bh, mixed. | Rally using both strokes—free choice | 50 |
| *Dropshots* | (2 steps into the centre after each shot. Move quickly and get behind the shuttle.) | |
| 5. Fh. dropshot. | A 10 fh drops—B feed A continuously. | 10 |
| 6. ,, | Change over. | 10 |
| 7. Bh. dropshot. | Repeat and for the fh. | 10 |
| 8. ,, | Change over | 10 |
| 9. Drop rally. | A serve high. B drop. A net return. B clear high. A drop. B net return. A clear high, and continue until each player had hit 10 drops each. | |
| *Smash* | | |
| 10. | A smash. B backhand return. | 10 |
| 11. | Change over. | 10 |
| 12. | A smash. B forehand return. | 10 |
| 13. | Change over. | 10 |
| 14. Smash rally. | B serve high. A smash. B low return. A clear high. B smash. A low return, and continue until player has hit 10 smashes. | |
| Low return rally. | A and B in the half court stroking the shuttle to each other—skimming the net. | 20 |

# STROKE TRAINING PROGRAMME

*Name* A. BROWN    *Duration*    4 Weeks    *Dates*

| STROKE | PAGE | SEQ. NO. | wk 1 | wk 2 | wk 3 | wk 4 | wk 5 | wk 6 | wk 7 | wk 8 | COMMENTS |
|---|---|---|---|---|---|---|---|---|---|---|---|
| | | | | | | | REPETITIONS | | | | |
| 1. F'hand clear | 88 | 1 | 10 | 10 | 15 | 20 | | | | | |
| 2. F'hand clear | 93 | 9 | 10 | 10 | 15 | 20 | | | | | |
| 3. F'hand clear | 94 | 11 | 5 | 5 | 10 | 10 | | | | | |
| 4. F'hand dropshot | 109 | 8 | 10 | 10 | 15 | 20 | | | | | |
| 5. F'hand dropshot | 107 | 3 | 10 | 10 | 15 | 20 | | | | | |
| 6. B'hand      ,, | 118 | 2 | 10 | 10 | 10 | 10 | | | | | |
| 7. F'hand      ,, | 111 | 2 | 5 | 5 | 10 | 10 | | | | | |
| 8. Overhead and underarm clear | 98 | 3 | 5 | 5 | 10 | 15 | | | | | |
| 9.            ,, | 101 | 6 | 5 | 5 | 10 | 15 | | | | | |
| 10.           ,, | 103 | 8 | 5 | 5 | 10 | 10 | | | | | |
| Pressure training | 162 | | | | | | | | | | Feeder hit 25 from centre net and 25 from centre rearcourt. |

Conditioned singles 159 Fig 117

Normal singles

SHEET D

# TRAINING CHART

Name  A. BROWN          Duration  4 Weeks

| | EXERCISES | RUNNING | SKIPPING | STROKE PRACTICE | STROKE TRAINING | PLAY | COMMENTS |
|---|---|---|---|---|---|---|---|
| MONDAY | ✓ | ✓ ✓ | ✓ | ✓ | | | 1. |
| | X | ✓ | ✓ | X | | ✓ | 2. |
| | | | | | ✓ | ✓ | 3. Strained Muscle |
| TUESDAY | | ✓ ✓ | ✓ ✓ | | ✓ | ✓ | |
| | | | | | ✓ | ✓ | |
| WEDNESDAY | | ✓ ✓ | ✓ ✓ | ✓ ✓ | | ✓ | |
| | | | | | | ✓ | |
| THURSDAY | | ✓ ✓ | ✓ ✓ | ✓ | ✓ | | |
| | | | | | ✓ | | |
| FRIDAY | | ✓ ✓ | ✓ ✓ | ✓ ✓ | | | |
| | | | | | | | |
| SATURDAY | | | ✓ ✓ | ✓ | ✓ ✓ | ✓ | |
| | | | | | | | |
| SUNDAY | | | | | | | |

240

## 51. COACH AND PLAYER RELATIONSHIP

I have stated that each player is a unique individual in his own right. He is to be respected as a person with his own point of view. Badminton is that sort of game in which individuals are dependent solely on their own efforts once they go onto the court. The nature of the game, a battle of skill between two or four persons require that the player assumes the responsibility for making decisions on the court. He must be autonomous once he steps on the court. To play the game well and make appropriate decisions requires an understanding of the game and a knowledge of what he is about. What then are the implications for the coach?

Players do not need coaches. Coaches need players without whom they would be redundant. The programme is designed to suit the player and to improve his performance. It is the player that matters. The coach must tune in to the player. This is not to say that the coach is the servant of the player. The relationship is a mutual one with each member contributing in his own special way to a particular end. It is a relationship built upon mutual trust and honesty, without whieh it cannot function.

Players are necessarily concerned with the realisation of their ambition. To this extent they must be self-centred and single minded in the pursuit of their goal. The coach is valuable in this enterprise. But when the final test arrives all the responsibility rests with the player.

The coach's job is to get the player inside the game. To provide him with deeper understanding. He must promote questioning and discussion about the game. He must encourage the player to be independent and autonomous. To do this the coach cannot dominate the relationship and dictate to the player. Such characteristics arise from a relationship based on discussion between player and coach; in which each is respected as a person with his own point of view; in which the work and any development is considered and agreed upon by both coach and player. The ultimate aim is for the coach to make himself redundant.


## 52. A COACHING SESSION

There are many different ways of organising a coaching session. It is not possible to lay down a rigid order which must be followed at all times. The example offered below is based on a logical progression which takes into consideration physiological factors concerning exercise and psychological factors concerning learning and skill acquisition.

*Part 1:*
(a) *Warm-up.* The player will benefit if he has a simple exercise routine which he does prior to going on the court. One based mainly on stretching and loosening exercises which prepare the player for work. To work through the body from head to feet, stretching the limbs through their

241

range of movement. As much as is possible the exercises should be adapted from badminton movements.

(b) *Knock-up*. The player goes through a knock-up routine in which he becomes accustomed to the flight of the shuttle and air conditions. He develops his 'feel' for the shuttle and works his way into a state of readiness for more rigorous work. The knock-up will be a set routine. First, hitting the shuttles from the sides, underarm shots and overhead clears, smashes, and drops etc, from a stationary position. Second, repeating this with travelling. The knock-up performed efficiently need only take about thirty minutes.

(c) *Skill practice*. Work will involve a stroke practice routine with the emphasis on quality. This means moving quickly into position, good balance, weight behind the shuttle, good stylish stroke and then moving quickly back to base. The coach can demand standards in the practice. Performed with quality the work is quite tiring.

(d) *Stroke sequence routine*. This may take place instead of, or as well as the stroke practice.

*Part 2*. The second part of the session will be spent on working on some specific aspect of the game. This might be a simple lunge from the centre to play a jab shot at the net; or an advanced defensive base as a tactical move in doubles. This is the period when experimenting takes place and involves much discussion. The work is difficult and requires attention and preseverance from the player, and patience and understanding from the coach.

*Part 3*. The final part will be games play. Usually the players would play a conditioned game. They are compelled to perform the new work in a game situation. For example, assume a doubles pair have been working on methods of playing tight net returns in defence to gain the attack. The coach will condition the game so, that the doubles pair will not be allowed to clear from any underarm position. This will force them to play tight returns in all defensive situations.

To sum up:- The progression in the session involves three parts.

(1) Practise basic skills.

(2) Acquire new skills.

(3) Apply new skills in a game.


## 53. TOURNAMENT PLAY

In writing about tournament play it is recognised that badminton is still mainly an amateur sport. It is appreciated that badminton players must earn a living and so are not able to make ideal preparations for a tournament. In order to draw attention to all the factors involved in the preparation for tournaments it is assumed that the player is able to make the ideal preparations.

(A) PRE-TOURNAMENT PREPARATIONS

*Training:* Conclude training and practice to allow at least one full day for resting before the tournament. The body is allowed to recover from the rigours of training and attains a state of readiness for the event.

*Travel:* If the tournament is some distance away then it is advisable to travel to the venue early to allow for the rest period. Competitions held in another country present special problems to do with the effects of travelling. Specialist advice is required for these occasions.

*Accommodation:* Select accommodation which allows one the freedom to rest. This would imply a place which is quiet, away from traffic, and where one can be allowed to sleep late in the morning or during the day without disturbance. Freedom to rest in a quiet environment is essential to prevent unnecessary tensions.

*The venue:* If possible it is advisable to visit the courts the day before the tournament and have a short knock-up. This enables one to become familiar with the conditions i.e. lighting, draughts (if any), floor suface, and any features which are relevant to play.

(B) THE TOURNAMENT

*Opponents:* If you have made a file of opponents now is the time to study it. Check the draw for the possible opponents and then make a study of the first opponent.

*Equipment:* Is is a small detail but very important that one has sufficient equipment. It is also important that nothing is forgotten when packing. Here are some suggestions. Rackets: About three rackets are required for a tournament.

Footwear: Two pairs of shoes are essential. A spare pair is useful should one pair split. A change between matches is refreshing whereas continuous play in the same pair simply makes that pair damp from perspiration.

In addition extra socks, shirts for each match make a difference to personal comfort and the general feeling of well being. These are basic items of equipment. Some players also include such items as elastoplast, scissors, extra shoelaces, and carry all these items on the court with them for the game. It is attention to small details that prevents the occurrence of situations

243

|             | which may upset the player, and that reduces the possibility of stress. |
| *The venue:* | Arrive early. It is important to become acclimatised to the conditions in the hall. One must allow time to go through the 'ready to play' procedure, i.e. warm-up and knock-up. |
| *Dress:* | Warm-up and knock-up in a track suit. The important factor is to exercise the body and then keep it warm ready for a 'flying start' when the match begins. Tracksuits can be removed just prior to the game. |

(C) THE GAME

*The relationship of practice and competition:* In practice the player has been working on new ideas, to improve his skill and to develop his game. The tournament is the testing ground for the player. It would seem appropriate to make a concious effort to try out his ideas and new strokes in the tournament. Unfortunately any conscious effort to do so focuses the attention of the player on his strokes. He does so at the risk of losing the match, for once on the court he should concentrate on playing his opponent and not on playing his strokes. He should attend to his opponent and play those strokes appropriate to outwitting his opponent. The player should try to forget all about his practice and any new developments in his game. Surely if he has been learning new skills and new tactics his game will already have begun to change from what it once was? This is what is implied when we use the word 'learning'. He does not have to try to use his new skills, for to the extent that he has learnt them, and they have been incorporated into his game, so will he use them.

During a game a coach should attend and observe. It is in the competition that he can judge the amount of development. On the basis of his observations he can modify the programme accordingly. The tournament is the situation where the coach learns.

*Playing the game:* The player should play to win. What does this mean? It means to play to win each rally. A player trains to be able to play full out for the duration of the match. For this reason he should play each rally for its own sake and let the points take care of themselves. A player who wins the majority of rallies will win the game.

Players often get upset over wrong calls and bad decisions. It is human to become upset but unfortunately often detrimental to the player's performance. Remember it is also human to make wrong calls and bad decisions. Once a decision is made, rightly or wrongly, the rally is concluded and the score alters. Only the rally being played can affect the score. It is important to remember this point. A player should concentrate on the present rally, the one that counts, and not think of the previous one or future ones.

*End of the game:* After the normal courtesies to the opponent and the um-

244

pire, take your equipment and return directly to the changing room. Strip off the damp clothes, wash and dry, and change into fresh clothes. Most players do not do this immediately the game is concluded. Yet to stand around in sweaty clothes is unwise. First, the body is still warm and producing heat. This means that energy is being used and vital calories are used up. These are necessary for future games during the tournament. Second, as one cools down the clothes become cold and damp; muscles contract and the player starts to feel stiff. Unless he goes through a thorough warm-up session before playing again he might easily strain a muscle, or not perform as well as he could. Pay attention to the details and take care of the body.

*Evaluation:* The player and the coach learn much about their work from the competition. Any evaluation must take both individual points of view into consideration. The coach views the player's performance objectively, from the standpoint of a critic. The player examines his own performance objectively and subjectively. He can make certain objective appraisals according to the success or lack of success of certain moves. He also evaluates the game according to how he felt during it. If the moves which he made during the game felt right to him then he may feel satisfied with what he did. To look on critically from the outside qua coach and from the inside qua player are two sides of the same coin when any evaluation of the player's performance is made.

The coach and the player are advised to reflect on the competition. This usually takes time and is one reason why immediate assessment of a game is unwise. Both the player and the coach need time to 'play' the game over in the mind, and to give careful thought to what went on. Experience of working together in this way will usually decide when it is appropriate to do so.

The evaluation will involve a discussion centred on relevant questions. 'Why did you lose?' 'Why did you change tactics when leading 8–7 in the third game?' 'Do you know why your opponent caught you constantly with the sliced cross-court smash to the forehand?'

'You looked very quick on the court. Shall we leave the speed work alone now and concentrate on something else?'

'You seemed to attack in the forecourt so much that you committed yourself and could not cover the return. Do you think that we are doing too much work on that part? Shall we continue with it until you master it or leave it for a period?'

'I think that I should play a few more games in practice because I feel too concious of myself and not concious enough of my opponent. What do you think?'

Each person asks questions and both consider them and discuss the problems together. On the basis of such discussion, the programme is revised. They may continue with the work as previously planned or decide to ignore some of it and modify other parts. Then once more it is a return to the

245

discipline of the work and the striving for standards. The task, to improve performance and attain the target, success in competition.

## 54. CONCLUSION

I began this book by stating, 'Anyone can learn to play badminton' and 'Very little skill is required to hit the shuttlecock over the net and play a rally with a friend' (see page 9). In this sense badminton is a simple game. It becomes extremely complex because people are capable of attaining a high degree of skill and fitness, and a high level of thought in the activities which they pursue. The game does involve hitting a shuttle over a net and playing a rally. Yet the complexity of the situations which occur, make such demands on a player that he sometimes finds it difficult to play a rally let alone end one to his advantage.

There are all sorts of factors which contribute to make the game so very complex and so interesting to both players and spectators. The demands on the player to reach this level of play are great and require much hard work. I have tried to indicate what must be developed, i.e. skill and fitness, and how to acquire this, throughout this book. This has been simple enough when it is only a matter of providing instructions.

It has not been possible to provide instructions in the section on competition badminton. The human factor is of paramount importance in competition whether the player works alone or works with a coach. I have concentrated mainly on the player who works with a coach for at the top level of play this is often the case. I have tried to emphasise that there is a human relationship involved in the preparation, and it is the human aspect of the game which is important in the performance of the player. In this final part of the book I have tried to draw attention to and clarify just what features are involved.

If this section provides coaches and players with more insight into the game, helps them to make more effective use of parts 1 and 2 of the book, and improves the performance of the player, then it will have served its purpose.

# APPENDIX

## THE LAWS OF BADMINTON
as revised in the year 1939 and adopted by
### THE INTERNATIONAL BADMINTON FEDERATION
Subsequently revised up-to-date
(Reprinted by courtesy of The Badminton Association of England)

---

## COURT

1. (*a*) The court shall be laid out as in the following Diagram 'A' (except in the case provided for in paragraph (*b*) of this Law) and to the measurements there shown, and shall be defined by white or yellow lines or, if this is not possible, by other easily distinguishable lines, 1½ inches (4 cm) wide.

In marking the court, the width (1½ inches) (4 cm) of the centre lines shall be equally divided between the right and left service courts; the width (1½ inches each) (4 cm each) of the short service line and the long service line shall fall within the 13-feet (3.96 m) measurement given as the length of the service court; and the width (1½ inches each) (4 cm each) of all other boundary lines shall fall within the measurements given.

(*b*) Where space does not permit of the marking out of a court for doubles, a court may be marked out for singles only as shown in Diagram 'B'. The back boundary lines become also the long service lines, and the posts, or the strips of material representing them as referred to in Law 2, shall be placed on the side lines.

## POSTS

2. The posts shall be 5 feet 1 inch (1.55 m) in height from the surface of the court. They shall be sufficiently firm to keep the net strained as provided in Law 3, and shall be placed on the side boundary lines of the court. Where this is not practicable, some method must be employed for indicating the position of the side boundary line where it passes under the net, e.g. by the use of a thin post or strip of material not less than 1½ inches (4 cm) in width, fixed to the side boundary line and rising vertically to the net cord. Where this is in use on a court marked for doubles it shall be placed on the boundary line of the doubles court irrespective of whether singles or doubles are being played.

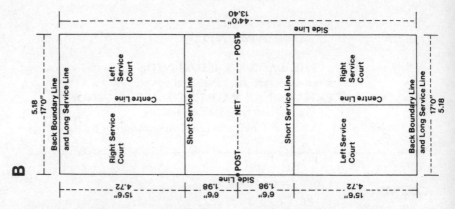

**B**

Diagonal Measurement of full Court 47ft. 2ins. (14.336 Metres)
" " of half Court 27ft. 9⅝ ins. (8.469 Metres) from Post to Back Boundary

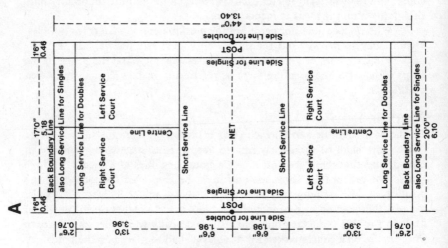

**A**

Diagonal Measurement of full Court 48ft. 4 ins. (14.723 Metres)
" " of half Court 29ft. 8¾ ins. (9.061 Metres) from Post to Back Boundary

248

## NET
3. The net shall be made of fine natural cord or artificial fibre of a dark colour and even thickness not exceeding ⅝ to ¾-inch (1.5 to 2 cm) mesh. It shall be firmly stretched from post to post, and shall be 2 feet 6 inches (0.76 m) in depth. The top of the net shall be 5 feet (1.524 m) in height from the floor at the centre, and 5 feet 1 inch (1.55 m) at the posts, and shall be edged with a 3 inch (75 mm) white tape doubled and supported by a cord or cable run though the tape and strained over and flush with the top of the posts.

## SHUTTLE
4. A shuttle shall weigh from 73 to 85 grains (4.73 to 5.50 gm), and shall have from 14 to 16 feathers fixed in a cork, 1 inch to 1⅛ inches (0.025 to 0.028 m) in diameter. The feathers shall be from 2½ to 2¾ inches (0.064 to 0.070 m) in length from the tip to the top of the cork base. They shall have from 2⅛ to 2½ inches (0.054 to 0.064 m) spread at the top and shall be firmly fastened with thread or other suitable material.

Subject to there being no substantial variation in the general design, pace, weight and flight of the shuttle, modifications in the above specifications may be made, subject to the approval of the National Organisation concerned.

(a) in places where atmospheric conditions, due either to altitude or climate, make the standard shuttle unsuitable; or

(b) if special circumstances exist which make it otherwise expedient in the interests of the game.

(*The Badminton Association of England has approved the use of modified shuttles (e.g. plastic, nylon, etc.), for play in England*).

A shuttle shall be deemed to be of correct pace if, when a player of average strength strikes it with a full underhand stroke from a spot immediately above one back boundary line in a line parallel to the side lines, and at an upward angle, it falls not less than 1 foot (0.30 m) and not more than 2 feet 6 inches (0.76 m) short of the other back boundary line.

## PLAYERS
5. (a) The word 'Player' applies to all those taking part in a game.

(b) The game shall be played, in the case of the doubles game, by two players a side, and in the case of the singles game, by one player a side.

(c) The side for the time being having the right to serve shall be called the 'In' side, and the opposing side shall be called the 'Out' side.

## THE TOSS
6. Before commencing play the opposing sides shall toss, and the side winning the toss shall have the option of:

(a) Serving first; or

(b) Not serving first, or

(c) Choosing ends.

249

The side losing the toss shall then have the choice of any alternative remaining.

SCORING

7. (a) The doubles and men's singles game consists of 15 or 21 points, as may be arranged. Provided that in a game of 15 points, when the score is 13-all, the side which first reached 13 has the option of 'Setting' the game to five, and that when the score is 14-all, the side which first reached 14 has the option of 'Setting' the game to 3. After the game has been 'Set' the score is called 'Love All' and the side which first scores 5 or 3 points, according as the game has been 'Set' at 13- or 14-all, wins the game. In either case the claim to 'Set' the game must be made before the next service is delivered after the score has reached 13-all or 14-all. Provided also that in a game of 21 points the same method of scoring be adopted, substituting 19 and 20 for 13 and 14.

(b) The ladies' singles game consists of 11 points, provided that when the score is '9-all' the player who first reached 9 has the option of 'Setting' the game to 3, and when the score is '10-all' the player who first reached 10 has the option of 'Setting' the game to 2.

(c) A side rejecting the option of 'Setting' at the first opportunity shall not be thereby barred from 'Setting' if a second opportunity arises.

(d) In handicap games 'Setting' is not permitted.

8. The opposing sides shall contest the best of three games, unless otherwise agreed. The players shall change ends at the commencement of the second game and also of the third game (if any). In the third game the players shall changes ends when the leading score reaches:

(a) 8 in a game of 15 points;

(b) 6 in a game of 11 points;

(c) 11 in a game of 21 points;

or, in handicap events, when one of the sides has scored half the total number of points required to win the game (the next highest number being taken in case of fractions). When it has been agreed to play only one game the players shall change ends as provided above for the third game.

If, inadvertently, the players omit to change ends as provided in this Law at the score indicated, the ends shall be changed immediately the mistake is discovered, and the existing score shall stand.

DOUBLES PLAY

9. (a) It having been decided which side is to have the first service, the player in the right-hand service court of that side commences the game by serving to the player in the service court diagonally opposite. If the latter player returns the shuttle before it touches the ground it is to be returned by one of the 'In' side, and then returned by one of the 'Out' side, and so on, until a fault is made or the shuttle ceases to be "In Play". (*Vide* paragraph (b). If

250

a fault is made by the "In" side, its rights to continue serving is lost as only one player on the side beginning a game is entitled to do so (*Vide* Law 11), and the opponent in the right-hand service court then becomes the server; but if the service is not returned, or the fault is made by the 'Out' side, the 'In' side scores a point. The 'In' side players then change from one service court to the other, the service now being from the left-hand service court to the player in the service court diagonally opposite. So long as a side remains 'In' service is delivered alternately from each service court into the one diagonally opposite, the change being made by the 'In' side when, and only when, a point is added to its score.

(*b*) The first service of a side in each innings shall be made from the right-hand service court. A 'Service' is delivered as soon as the shuttle is struck by the server's racket. The shuttle is thereafter 'In Play' until it touches the ground, or until a fault or 'Let' occurs, or except as provided in Law 19. After the service is delivered, the server and the player served to may take up any positions they choose on their side of the net, irrespective of any boundary lines.

10. The player served to may alone receive the service, but should the shuttle touch, or be struck by, his partner the 'In' side scores a point. No player may receive two consecutive services in the same game, except as provided in Law 12.

11. Only one player of the side beginning a game shall be entitled to serve in its first innings. In all subsequent innings each partner shall have the right, and they shall serve consecutively. The side winning a game shall always serve first in the next game, but either of the winners may serve and either of the losers may receive the service.

12. If a player serves out of turn, or from the wrong service court (owing to a mistake as to the service court from which service is at the time being in order), *and his side wins the rally*, it shall be a 'Let' provided that such 'Let' be claimed or allowed before the next succeeding service is delivered.

If a player of the 'Out' side, standing in the wrong service court is prepared to receive the service when it is delivered, *and his side wins the rally*, it shall be a 'Let', provided that such 'Let' be claimed and allowed, or ordered by the umpire, before the next succeeding service is delivered.

If in either of the above cases the side at fault *loses the rally*, the mistake shall stand and the players' positions shall not be corrected.

Should a player inadvertently change sides when he should not do so, and the mistake not be discovered until after the next succeeding service has been delivered, the mistake shall stand, and a 'Let' cannot be claimed or allowed, and the players positions shall not be corrected.

SINGLES PLAY

13. In singles Laws 9 and 12 hold good, except that:

251

(a) The players shall serve from and receive service in their respective right-hand service courts only when the server's score is 0 or an even number of points in the game, the service being delivered from and received in their respective left-hand service courts when the server's score is an odd number of points.

(b) Both players shall change service courts after each point has been scored.

## FAULTS

14. A fault made by a player of the side which is 'In' puts the server out; if made by a player whose side is 'Out', it counts a point to the 'In' side.

It is a fault:

(a) If in serving, (i) the shuttle at the instant of being struck be higher than the server's waist, or (ii) if at the instant of the shuttle being struck the shaft of the racket be not pointing in a downward direction to such an extent that the whole of the head of the racket is discernably below the whole of the server's hand holding the racket.

(b) If, in serving, the shuttle does not pass over the net, or falls into the wrong service court (i.e., into the one not diagonally opposite to the server), or falls short of the short service line, or beyond the long service line, or outside the side boundary lines of the service court into which service is in order.

(c) If the server's feet are not in the service court from which service is at the time being in order, or if the feet of the player receiving the service are not in the service court diagonally opposite until the service is delivered. (*Vide* Law 16).

(d) If before or during the delivery of the service any player makes preliminary feints or otherwise intentionally baulks his opponent, or if any player deliberately delays serving the shuttle or in getting ready to receive it so as to obtain an unfair advantage.

(e) If either in service or play, the shuttle falls outside the boundaries of the court, or passes through or under the net, or fails to pass the net, or touches the roof or side walls, or the person or dress of a player. (A shuttle falling on a line shall be deemed to have fallen in the court or service court of which such line is a boundary).

(f) If the shuttle 'In Play' be struck before it crosses to the striker's side of the net. (The striker may, however, follow the shuttle over the net with his racket in the course of his stroke).

(g) If, when the shuttle is 'In Play', a player touches the net or its support with racket, person or dress.

(h) If the shuttle be held on the racket (i.e. caught or slung) during the execution of a stroke; or if the shuttle be hit twice in succession by the same player with two strokes; or if the shuttle be hit by a player and his partner successively.

(i) If, in play, a player strikes the shuttle (unless he thereby makes a good return) or is struck by it, whether he is standing within or outside the boundaries of the court.

(j) If a player obstructs an opponent.

(k) If Law 16 be transgressed.

## GENERAL

15. The server may not serve until his opponent is ready, but the opponent shall be deemed to be ready if a return of the service be attempted.

16. The server and the player served to must stand within the limits of their respective courts (as bounded by the short and long service, the centre, and side lines) and some part of both feet of these players must remain in contact with the ground in a stationary position until the service is delivered. A foot on or touching a line in the case of either the server or the receiver shall be held to be outside his service court. (*Vide* Law 14(c).) The respective partners may take up any position, provided they do not unsight or otherwise obstruct an opponent.

17. (a) If, in the course of service or rally, the shuttle touches and passes over the net the stroke is not invalidated thereby. It is a good return if the shuttle having passed outside either post drops on or within the boundary lines of the opposite court. A 'Let' may be given by the umpire for any unforeseen or accidental hindrance.

(b) If, in service, or during a rally, a shuttle *after passing over the net, is caught in or on the net*, it is a 'Let'.

(c) If the receiver is faulted for moving before the service is delivered, or for not being within the correct service court, in accordance with Laws 14(c) or 16, and at the same time the server is also faulted for a service infringement, it shall be a let.

(d) When a 'Let' occurs, the play since the last service shall not count, and the player who served shall serve again, except when Law 12 is applicable.

18. If the server, in attempting to serve, misses the shuttle, it is not a fault; but if the shuttle be touched by the racket, a service is thereby delivered.

19. If when in play, the shuttle strikes the net and remains suspended there, or strikes the net and falls towards the ground on the striker's side of the net, or hits the ground outside the court and an opponent then touches the net or shuttle with his racket or person, there is no penalty, as the shuttle is not then in play.

20. If a player has a chance of striking the shuttle in a downward direction when quite near the net, his opponent must not put up his racket near the

253

net on the chance of the shuttle rebounding from it. This is obstruction within the meaning of Law 14(*j*).

A player may, however, hold up his racket to protect his face from being hit if he does not thereby baulk his opponent.

21. It shall be the duty of the umpire to call 'Fault' or 'Let' should either occur, without appeal being made by the players and to give his decision on any appeal regarding a point in dispute, if made before the next service; and also to appoint linesmen and service judges at his discretion. The umpire's decision shall be final, but he shall uphold the decision of a linesman or service judge. This shall not preclude the umpire also from faulting the server or receiver. Where, however, a referee is appointed, an appeal shall lie to him from the decision of an umpire on questions of law only.

## CONTINUOUS PLAY

22. Play shall be continuous from the first service until the match be concluded; except that (*a*) in the International Badminton Championship and in the Ladies' International Badminton Championship there shall be allowed an interval not exceeding five minutes between the second and third games of a match; (*b*) in countries where climatic conditions render it desirable, there shall be allowed, subject to the previously published approval of the National Organisation concerned, an interval not exceeding five minutes between the second and third games of a match, in singles or doubles, or both; and (*c*) when necessitated by circumstances not within the control of the players, the umpire may suspend play for such a period as he may consider necessary. If play be suspended the existing score shall stand and play be resumed from that point. Under no circumstances shall play be suspended to enable a player to recover his strength or wind, or to receive instruction or advice. Except in the case of any interval already provided for above, no player shall be allowed to receive advice during a match or to leave the court until the match be concluded without the umpire's consent. The umpire shall be the sole judge of any suspension of play and he shall have the right to disqualify any offender.

(*The Badminton Association of England has sanctioned that there may be an interval not exceeding five minutes between the second and third games only in matches in International Fixtures in England, subject to the agreement of the opponents.*)

## INTERPRETATIONS

1. Any movement or conduct by the server that has the effect of breaking the continuity of service after the server and receiver have taken their positions to serve and to receive the service is a preliminary feint. For example, a server, who after having taken up his position to serve, delays hitting the shuttle for so long as to be unfair to the receiver, is guilty of such conduct.

254

(*Vide* Law 14(*d*).)

2. It is obstruction if a player invades an opponent's court with racket or person in any degree except as permitted in Law 14 (*f*).

(*Vide* Law 14(*j*).)

3. Where necessary on account of the structure of a building, the local Badminton Authority may, subject to the right of veto of its National Organisation, make bye-laws dealing with cases in which a shuttle touches an obstruction.

255